A practical self-help guide to recovery from
burnout & restoring well-being

The 5 Keys
to
Burnout
Recovery

Dr. Catherine Buchan

First published in the United Kingdom in 2021

Published by The Agile Leader Limited.

Visit: www.thecompassiondoctor.com

TABLE OF CONTENTS

ACKNOWLEDGEMENTS

My heartfelt thanks to: my parents Ray and Pam Parry and my brother James Parry for their support; to my uncle John Carey for his contribution; to Jenny Collins, Alison Shah, Sietske Harmsen and Sarah Mowatt for their friendship and support and especially for their enthusiasm and encouragement during the writing of this book.

Special thanks go to Dr. Claire Parkes, not only for her friendship and support, but also for making the time in her incredibly busy life to read the draft of this book and provide me with her invaluable feedback.

Additionally, I would like to thank all the researchers who have investigated the experience of burnout and restoring well-being. I would also like to thank all the health professionals, who are too numerous to mention, for their support and assistance during my burnout and recovery experiences.

Finally, I dedicate this book to my wonderful husband Mark, without whom this book would not have been possible. I would like to thank him for his endless support, patience and encouragement throughout the writing of this book. Thanks for cooking me all those delicious meals, for making me laugh, for your great coaching, for reading the initial drafts and for the publishing of the final version. I am so deeply grateful to you Mark. Thank you from the bottom of my heart.

PREFACE

Employ your time in improving yourself by other men's [or women's!] writings so that you shall gain easily what others have laboured hard for.

Socrates

Burnout is a growing global problem with many negative consequences. It costs organisations (absenteeism, turnover, extra pressure on other employees who remain in work, for example) and it has many negative impacts on those suffering from burnout, not just in terms of our mental health, but also our physical well-being, our interpersonal relationships and our social lives. It impacts our ability to do our jobs, affecting our performance and it can ultimately cost us our careers too, as it did for me, not once but twice, firstly in the travel industry, and secondly in healthcare. In addition, burnout is a complex issue, without one agreed definition, and numerous factors are attributed to its cause. This is compounded by the problem that we may not even realise that what we are suffering from is actually burnout. Alternatively, we might realise it but ignore what our body is trying to tell us and continue to keep pushing ourselves, until we are no longer able to function. I personally experienced both of these parts of the burnout process, as have others, as I reveal in this book.

Given all of the above, it is no surprise that there is a plethora of research investigating the causes of burnout and how to try and prevent it. Initially, I wanted to add to this body of work by writing a book on how to prevent burnout, drawing on all that I have learned from having experienced it twice, especially regarding the warning signs. In the process of researching for that book, I discovered much less is known about how to recover from burnout and that, in comparison with prevention, it is an under-researched area. What is known so far is that for people who are experiencing mild or low levels of burnout, it may be relatively easy to recover, by taking some time out to rest, recharge, do some self-care, for example.

However, for those experiencing more severe work-related burnout, sometimes referred to as "clinical burnout" (Shaufeli et al., 2001), the research, and my own experiences, show that it requires more to recover, sometimes making some significant changes, that it is a process and it takes time. What I also discovered, which motivated me even further, was that it has been reported that burnout cannot be overcome using one specific treatment (Lapa et al., 2017). I too found I could not recover from it using one particular intervention. Similarly, both times I managed to recover from burnout I did so without following a specific "road map" and instead intuitively, and through trial and error, devised my own. Consequently, I felt compelled to change the aim of the book by focusing on burnout recovery instead, so that others can benefit from what I have learned and my experiences and, in effect, have a "road map", in the form of the five keys that I reveal in this book.

Burnout is complex and trying to recover can be too. Therefore, the benefit of this book is that it focuses on what is important, what helps recovery, rather than providing an in-depth account of everything related to the subject of burnout. Hence, I have designed this book to be a quick and easy read, and as simple to implement as possible, because that is what I would have found so helpful when I was suffering from burnout. Another benefit of reading this book is that in Part One, it reveals the five keys to recovery, which provide readers who are experiencing burnout with a road map which will assist them in burnout recovery and restoring their well-being. These five keys are not only based on my personal experiences, but are also supported by the research, so they are evidence-based.

Additionally, the focus of each key is on what is important and why it is important in the recovery process, with some tips on how to get started with each one, rather than a detailed description of how to implement each one. This is also because the severity of the level of burnout differs from person to person, as do our needs and other related factors. It took me a number of years to recover from burnout both times. Consequently, another benefit of this book is that it can potentially help speed up the process of recovery too, so others can gain more easily, and more quickly, what I had to work relatively long and hard for.

A further benefit of reading this book is that, in addition to the five keys, in Part Two, I provide an open and authentic account of my own experiences of burnout for readers to learn from. This includes the warning signs, the suffering I experienced and challenges of finding my own way out of it and back to well-being. Similarly, the benefit of the way the book is written is readers can pick and choose what they are most motivated to read about, or are able to process at any given time, according to their own levels of burnout, starting with Part Two if exhaustion levels are high, for example, or Part One if they are eager and able to begin their own recovery process.

Moreover, I am passionate about teaching people tools and strategies to improve their well-being and their lives. In the writing of this book, I have drawn on this passion, in addition to over 15 years in the field of psychology, that is: my knowledge, skills and experience I have gained through professional and personal development (personal therapy included), along with my work delivering therapy and coaching, running workshops and development groups and so on, as a change facilitator. This has all helped me to have further insights into my own journey and reach the point where I could communicate this to others in this book, with the aim of it being informative and inspiring to those trying to recover from burnout.

Finally, this book does not ignore that there are organisational factors that play a part in the cause of burnout, but it instead focuses on the one area where we have total control, that is ourselves. By working on ourselves, we are then in a better position mentally, emotionally and physically, to either try and implement changes within our organisations, or to know if it is time to change jobs or careers, as I did.

INTRODUCTION

The secret of change is to focus all your energy not on fighting the old, but on building the new.

Socrates

A brief overview of burnout

Given our current work culture, and how frequently it is discussed in the media, it might appear that burnout is a recent (21st Century) phenomenon. But an American psychologist, Freudenberger, is credited with developing the term "burnout" as far back as 1974. The concept was later developed further by Maslach and Jackson, who subsequently created the work-related burnout measure for use within the human service industry, known as the Maslach Burnout Inventory (MBI) (Maslach, Jackson & Leiter, 1996). Other measures of burnout have since been developed, including the Copenhagen Burnout Inventory (CBI) (Kristensen, Borritz, Villadsen & Christensen, 2005), which has the advantage of being able to be applied to occupations outside of the human service industry.

Research into burnout has grown substantially over the years, particularly in regard to investigating its causes and symptoms. Although the causes of burnout are still being explored, it is known that certain factors are linked to the development of burnout from both a personal, individual perspective, which is the focus of this book, and from the perspective of the environment, in this case, the workplace. It is also now established that burnout contributes to ill health and vice versa (Maslach & Leiter, 2016). Previously, it was perceived that there was one type of work-related burnout but, more recently, three different types of job-related burnout have been identified in the literature, namely "frenetic", "underchallenged" and "worn-out" (Montero-Marín et al., 2011).

Additionally, the number of people suffering from burnout has also increased over the years. It has become such a significant problem globally that in 2019 the World Health Organization (WHO) included a more detailed definition of it in its 11th Revision of the International Classification of Diseases (ICD-11). Work-related burnout is defined as a syndrome that occurs as a result of "chronic workplace stress that has not been successfully managed" (WHO, 2019). It is described as consisting of three aspects, namely "feelings of energy depletion or exhaustion", "increased mental distance from one's job, or feelings of negativism or cynicism related to one's job" and "reduced professional efficacy", and although it is within the "Classification of Diseases", it is not considered a medical condition (WHO, 2019). Hence, when I refer to "burnout" in this book, I am referring to the definition and description as specified by the WHO (2019), for simplicity.

The burnout problem
Rates of burnout are increasing, as mentioned. The number of people with burnout in the UK was reported to be 57%, compared to 50% in the USA, 37% in Spain and 30% in Germany and France (Source: World Economic Forum October 2019). Burnout can be experienced by people working in any field, with numbers particularly high for those working in healthcare and education, for example. There is no existing calculation of the worldwide economic cost of burnout itself, but a related cost is that of mental illness, which is purported to grow to an estimated $16 trillion by 2030, which is believed to be related to the rise in the numbers of burnout cases (Cassar & Breitinger, 2019). These figures were of course all before the Covid-19 pandemic, which has made the problem even worse.

To experience burnout means that we have not been experiencing optimum "work–life balance", rather it reflects an imbalance of much more time spent on work activities than non-work activities, which can not only cause burnout, but can lead to other health issues, as mentioned. An investigation into "work–life balance" using information gathered from the 2010 European Working Conditions Survey (which included over 24,000 employees from 27 European countries), found that those who reported a poor "work–life balance" reported more health issues too (Lunau, Bambra, Eikemo, van der Wel & Dragano, 2014).

However, I, like some others, am personally not a fan of the term "work–life balance". Work is a part of life, not separate from it, for people that do work. There are other terms used sometimes, such as "work–family balance" or "work–non-work balance" (Casper, Vaziri, Wayne, DeHauw & Greenhaus, 2018). I do not like to use the term "work–family balance" either. It does not reflect my first burnout experience at all because, at that time, I was not in a significant intimate relationship, nor did I have any children, and nor did I particularly value spending time with my family!

No phrase perfectly reflects for me how I perceive this challenging "dance" with balance in life, that encompasses all that we have to do, or want to do, as adults. Even if we are able to reduce our time spent at work for example, we often do not make time in our non-work time for activities that enhance our resilience, happiness and well-being. Instead, we prioritise other activities, which may be essential (such as feeding ourselves, our children and pets) but equally they may not be (such as dusting and hoovering our own home every day). In my childhood, a famous confectionery company used to use the slogan "work, rest and play" in one of their advertising campaigns, which I think is a little more useful, as it includes play, which is an important aspect of recovery, as I explain in Part One. So, for the sake of ease, and without a more suitable alternative, I will continue to borrow from Casper et al. (2018) and use the term "work–non-work balance" in this book.

Another problem with burnout, especially as it often conflates with other health problems, is that we may not even realise what we are suffering from is burnout, as I personally found. The problem is compounded by the fact that there is no objective test for burnout, only self-reported, and thus subjective, measures. My first experience overlapped with other health conditions, which the GP diagnosed as Chronic Fatigue Syndrome (CFS) and coeliac disease. When I experienced what became the second burnout, I suspected that, on reflection, I may have also been suffering from it all those years previously, when I had to leave my travel career. However, I only became certain as I was researching this book.

I had wanted to include a questionnaire at the end of this book for readers to be able to assess if they were burnt out, and if so, what their level of burnout was. Although many of the assessment measures used in burnout research are not freely available, I did manage to discover a simple questionnaire that I could access (see Post, 1981). As I read through each question, I began to think "this reminds me of how I felt just before I had to leave my first career in the travel industry". So, I took the opportunity to complete the questionnaire, transporting myself back to that time. Imagine my shock when my total score (128) revealed that I was (or had been) in the highest category (91 and above)! This indicated that I had most likely been heading for what they described as "an advanced stage of burnout"! I completed the questionnaire again, thinking back to the time just before I left my second career in healthcare. The score was 107, again, within the highest category. This confirmed to me that whatever other health issues I had been experiencing during those two periods, I was definitely suffering from burnout too! Just for the fun of it, I re-did the questionnaire once more, for the present time, as I work to complete this book. I scored 36, within the lowest category (28–38), reflecting how much better I am doing now! (If you would like to complete the questionnaire for free, email me at cb@thecompassiondoctor.com for a copy).

Taking charge of your well-being

Even though burnout is a significant problem that is currently increasing globally, as previously mentioned, the good news is that it is possible to recover from it and restore our resilience. In relation to this, the overall message of this book, and what has been revealed in the psychology literature as one of the main themes that are important for burnout recovery, is to take charge of our well-being (e.g. Fjellman-Wiklund et al., 2010). Taking charge of my well-being is something I intuitively did to recover the first time, when, as I have said, it was not even recognised that I had burnout. The well-meaning medical professionals I saw at that time told me little was known about CFS, including how to help me overcome it, nor did they know if I even would be able to overcome it.

Consequently, the choice I had was to accept what they had told me or to do something I had never done before and take responsibility and control for my health and well-being, do research, experiment and do what I could to recover. I chose the latter thankfully, and successfully recovered. With regard to the second burnout, I had neglected my own well-being in favour of prioritising work and achieving a goal. Thus, once my contract ended, I took charge of my well-being once more and made the decision not to accept the renewal that was offered to me, choosing to begin the recovery process instead. Hence, another reason for me writing this book is to share this essential aspect of recovery with others.

How this book is organised

This book is divided into two main parts. Part One reveals the five keys to overcoming work-related burnout and restoring well-being to enable you to have the tools to begin the essential aspect of recovery, taking charge of your well-being. Part Two is an authentic account of my personal journey from resilience to burnout and back again, twice! The book is set out in this way with the five keys first, because I consider these to be the most important element of the book. This is because they include very useful information on what is helpful, and why it is so, for burnout recovery and restoring well-being, information that is not just based on my experience, but also supported by research. There is great value in reading other people's accounts of burnout too, because they can help us understand ourselves and have insights into our own experiences, which is why I have included mine. Nevertheless, they are often of secondary importance, due to their subjective nature and because individual burnout levels and experiences differ so much.

With regard to Part One, each key is divided into sections, to make it as simple and easy to read as possible. Each key starts with the topic in question and includes some other related concepts. Then I explain how the key is related to my first and second burnout recoveries, and how I benefited from them. Subsequently, each key includes a "Research Box" which includes evidence from psychological research into the experiences of people who have recovered from burnout and/or into what enhances well-being, providing support for the effectiveness of each key, for those who are interested in that. Finally, at the end of each key, I provide the reader with some simple tips to get started with how to apply the key in their life.

Although the keys can be read and applied in any order, I recommend starting with the first key, as it lays the foundation for those that follow. I have provided everything in this book that I used in my recoveries, but that does not mean the reader has to do everything I include too, because, as I mentioned, some people experience only mild burnout, and so can recover relatively easily with some time out from work and some basic self-care. Alternatively, others experience more severe burnout, and may need to do more to recover, as I did. Therefore, experiment with the keys. Each person needs to find out what works best for them, in their given situation, context and so on. Furthermore, even if you want to apply all the keys, you do not need to do them all at once! Take the time you need for each one, so that the process feels manageable.

In Part Two I provide readers with a detailed, authentic account of my personal experience of burnout and recovery. It starts with some information on my family background, which is pertinent to my experience, and then reveals how experiencing chronic stress subsequently resulted in burnout, not just once, but twice. I also share some of the biggest challenges I faced along the way to recovery, including accepting, and grieving, the loss of another career, albeit an emerging one. I do so with the aim of reassuring others suffering from burnout that they are not alone and that it may assist them in their own recovery, in the way that reading about others' experiences of ill health and other life challenges has inspired and helped me over the years.

It is of course not possible to cover everything that every single person who experiences burnout needs to recover in one book, and especially a book designed to be simple and easy to read and follow, to help those who are experiencing severe burnout, because – as is indicated in the literature – there are different causes of burnout, and different symptoms and we have different needs. So, the purpose of this book is to provide vital information on what is important, and why it is important, with regard to taking charge of your own well-being and recovering from burnout, and to help you kick-start the process.

PART ONE: THE 5 KEYS TO BURNOUT RECOVERY

KEY ONE: RAISE YOUR AWARENESS

Know thyself, for once we know ourselves, we may learn how to care for ourselves.

Socrates

Why raising your awareness is important for burnout recovery

The first, and essential measure, on this recovery path is raising our awareness, so that we can begin the change process. Without it, we are like a ship without a rudder, drifting endlessly "at sea", with no end in sight, to our burnout problem. It is, as Socrates' words reflect, essential in order for us to care for ourselves, to recover from burnout and enhance well-being, which is what this book is about. The limited research that has been carried out into burnout recovery has found that raising awareness, such as awareness of burnout symptoms, and the effects of stress on the body for example, in addition to self-awareness, has been an essential part of the recovery process (see Research Box). Additionally, self-awareness is perceived to be an important aspect of psychological well-being and essential for Emotional Intelligence (EI) too (see below) both of which help with regard to recovery and maintaining well-being.

What is self-awareness?

Self-awareness is complex and multidimensional (Morin, 2011). There are, as with many psychological concepts, differing perspectives about what it means exactly. However, in general, it means to consciously know what we are thinking and feeling, what our needs are, what is important to us, what gives our life meaning and brings us joy, for example. Because self-awareness involves recognising emotions in ourselves, as well as in others, it is perceived as an essential aspect of EI (Goleman, 2001b). Another aspect of self-awareness, also said to be linked to EI, is being aware of our strengths and limitations (Kooker, et al., 2007). Additionally, self-awareness, and particularly raising self-awareness, is one of the six dimensions that are purported to be a part of psychological well-being, described in this instance within the category of "personal growth" (Ryff, 1995).

Prior to my first burnout, I had what I describe in my first book as a "surface" level of self-awareness (Buchan, 2008). I was aware of my likes and dislikes in general, with regard to food, activities and people! I knew I had a high metabolism then and did not have to watch how much food I ate, as I never put on weight. I was aware I felt afraid of sleeping alone after the flat I was living in was burgled. I was aware I liked to please people, that I did not like conflict and would do what I could to avoid it. I was aware I had relationship problems (as I describe in Part Two).

As I reached burnout, I was aware I had work-related problems. I was aware I would burst into tears in my office at the slightest thing, with no idea as to why. I knew I was afraid the phone would ring, or I would receive more emails as it meant more work, but that had not been a problem before. I had no idea why it had become a problem. My emotions were overwhelming me, and I felt powerless to stop them. Additionally, I knew I felt something uncomfortable, an instant automatic emotional response, when someone at work said something that triggered me. It felt as though other people controlled my emotions. I would blame them for "making me" feel bad. This resulted in a sense of helplessness and powerlessness.

I was not aware of my thoughts, emotions and other behaviours, particularly those relating to stress and implicated in my burnout experience. I was not consciously aware I was treating myself like a machine, neglecting my fundamental needs, for example. I did not know I had workaholic and perfectionist tendencies, or the negative impact of these on me (see section on workaholism). Similarly, if you had asked me then what were the things that made me feel sustained or recharged, and what made me feel drained and depleted, I would not have been able to answer. There was so much more I came to realise that I had been unaware of, and how useful, even essential, awareness was to recovery, because, as the saying goes, you do not know what you do not know!

The importance of raising your self-awareness
Raising awareness of ourselves (our thoughts, emotions, bodily sensations, needs, values, etc.) is important with regard to recovery from burnout and it is fundamental to the other keys. This includes becoming aware of how we have been treating our body and what it really needs, so that we can restore our body, which is the subject of the second key; identifying our core values so that we can discover or rediscover meaning in our lives, in addition to identifying what is

11

important to us with regard to personal rights, as part of the third key, which is being true to ourselves.

Additionally, while raising awareness has many benefits and is fundamental to change, it can also be a double-edged sword. Once we become aware of something, we cannot go back to being unaware of it! We can find ourselves, once we start to raise our awareness of our thoughts, emotions, behaviours, limitations and so on, blaming ourselves, being self-critical, or not feeling able to make changes at work that would have helped us not reach that point, for example, and it may foster other negative thoughts.

Thus, whether we are conscious that we are doing it or not, it is natural for us to want to avoid raising our awareness. We do so by using avoidant coping strategies (which can include turning to food, alcohol, drugs or excessive busyness, for example), and denying that our bodies are suffering, that is, until we reach the point where we are experiencing more suffering than we are able to stand, sometimes described as a threshold, as I experienced.

Raising our awareness means we have to stop denying (at least to ourselves) that we are struggling, that we are exhausted, and instead admit that something has to change, and so we start the recovery process. This can be challenging, for many reasons, including the fact it shines a light on how badly we have been treating ourselves, and other factors, which can in turn lead to self-blame and so on.

Therefore, the final keys assist with this potential aspect of raising awareness, along with the facilitation of burnout recovery, that is, recognising if we lack self-acceptance and are self-critical, so that we can develop self-acceptance and self-compassion, as part of being kind to ourselves, which is the particular aim of the fourth key. Finally, it encompasses becoming aware of what makes us feel heartfelt joy, and identify if we have been neglecting leisure and social activities, so that we can choose activities that make our heart sing, the subject of the fifth key.

My first burnout recovery
At the time of my first burnout, I had not had therapy or coaching and had only experienced meditation very briefly as part of a yoga course, hence my level of self-awareness. Therefore, raising my awareness was a very big learning curve for me. I had wanted to have therapy for a long time prior to this point, more to help with my

relationship difficulties, but had always been too afraid to do so. It was not common practice amongst my family, circle of friends or colleagues to seek professional help at that time. Thankfully, there is much less of a stigma attached to this now. Nevertheless, I recognised I needed help by then, and I was eager to experience what it was like as a client, before I started my re-training in psychology.

My first therapist was a Gestalt therapist. This is not often the first form of therapy that is recommended, I later found out, as it can feel quite challenging for those not used to being in therapy. However, this therapist lived the closest to me, and that was important at that time, due to my energy challenges. I also found I really took to this type of therapy, finding the work with 'parts' and parts conflict, a key aspect of Gestalt theory, especially helpful. I later went on to include this aspect of Gestalt theory when I began working with clients, and I still incorporate it into client work, in addition to applying it to myself as part of my own personal change work.

To demonstrate how therapy helped me with raising awareness at that time, I include an excerpt from my first book, describing the experience:

> *The therapist was able to help me to see things about myself and my behaviours that I had been blind to [i.e. raising awareness; insights]. She helped me to understand why I had made the choices I had...I began to see that I had neglected my needs for a long time, and I came to understand why I had treated myself so badly and the effect it had. It was a relief to be able to change and begin to create a new life for myself. (Buchan, 2008; pg. 76)*

Another tool I used to help me raise my self-awareness was journaling, that is, recording events, situations and my thoughts, feelings and bodily sensations in relation to them, in a notebook. After each therapy session I recorded what we discussed in the session and, in particular, things that I wanted to remember that were especially insightful, and other aspects which would help me to subsequently implement changes in my life. Having therapy helped me with regard to journaling as it also provided me with a "safe container". This enabled me to feel safe enough to face the thoughts and emotions that would emerge in between sessions, knowing they would not overwhelm me, as the therapist taught me how to effectively manage my emotions.

Obviously, I had to pay for therapy, and I was using my savings for that. So, I looked for other ways to increase my self-awareness. I found watching a particular TV show very helpful for my personal development, and reading self-help books, as this extract from my first book reveals, at a time before we all had a home computer!

> In addition to psychotherapy [i.e., support] I watched many Oprah Winfrey TV shows and followed the advice of the experts that appeared on the show. When I had the energy, I devoured self-help books too...and carried out the exercises. (Buchan, 2008; pg.76)

An alternative health practitioner I had a session with to help restore my body, as I describe in the second key, recommended meditation to me and so I bought a CD on it and learnt how to do it. Practising meditation became an important part of raising my awareness, and maintaining my well-being, that continues to this day. All these factors resulted in me discovering through personal experience how important it is to make time for self-reflection, to raise our awareness.

A note of caution regarding raising our awareness and practising self-reflection, that is noticing our thoughts, how we are feeling emotionally, about ourselves, our situation and so on. This can sometimes, especially in the beginning when we are new to this practice, and if we are doing this on our own without the support of a therapist or coach, lead us to ruminate. To ruminate means to repeatedly and endlessly go over a thought or problem (Joireman, Parrott & Hammersla, 2002). This can lower our mood and keep us feeling stuck. Therefore, if we notice we are ruminating, we can just take a break from working on this key and move on to one of the other keys. The fifth and final key, make your heart sing, can be very useful.

Seeking some professional support can also help with this, as I discovered. When I had gained some useful insights through therapy, journaling and so on, but was still not feeling fully recovered, I also had a few sessions with a practitioner who did Neuro-linguistic Programming (NLP), coaching and hypnotherapy. I found the sessions so helpful that I went on to do his accredited course to qualify in this too. The aspects of this that I found particularly useful were that, unlike my therapy sessions, in parts of these sessions we stood up and the practitioner helped me to raise my awareness of how my posture was and what I was thinking and feeling in that moment as I stood a certain way. He then got me to change postures and notice what was different about my thoughts and my feelings. It was very effective. This was several years before I had discovered mindfulness!

My second burnout recovery

By the time I experienced the second burnout, many years had passed, many years of personal and professional development, including becoming a qualified psychologist, helping others raise their awareness and overcome their challenges, and much mediation and mindfulness practice. Thus, a lack of self-awareness per se, was not the issue with regard to the second burnout.

This time, the aspects of awareness that I needed to focus on for my recovery were to work out, through reflection, what could I have done to prevent the burnout, in addition to working out what I did (or neglected to do), that contributed to it (aside from what was very obvious to me, which was that I had neglected my well-being again, in favour of work – see *'A note on workaholism'*. Although I had been aware that I had been neglecting my meditation/mindfulness practice during the period leading up to the burnout, I had not been willing to admit to myself how important that was with regard to my stress management and maintaining my well-being. I had been so overwhelmed by the workload and all my other commitments, that I could not have admitted it to myself at that time as I felt unable to make time for it. I am now fully aware that for me personally, it is a vital part of my self-care, as I describe in some of the other keys.

Additionally, as part of my recovery, I had to admit to myself that I had neglected my core values in favour of other work-related values, as I explain in the third key. Similarly, I became very aware that, once again, my life had become very out of balance as I had also prioritised work over spending time on making my heart sing, which is apparent in the fifth key. Once I allowed myself to face my reality and how I had allowed myself to reach this point again, I had to work on forgiving myself, accepting and being compassionate towards myself for it, as I explain in detail in the fourth key. My recovery also included readdressing this imbalance of prioritising work over everything else, which I had by then realised, I had been driven to do for many years. This brings me to the subject of workaholism.

A note on workaholism

Workaholism is a big topic, which is beyond the scope of this book. However, I refer to it here briefly because there is a link between workaholism and burnout (Sussman, 2012). Additionally, an understanding of it has been useful regarding my recovery, and so, it may be helpful to others too. Workaholism involves both high levels of excessive working and high levels of compulsive working (Girardi, de Carlo, Andreassen & Falco, 2019). It involves being so preoccupied with work that it dominates our lives, and we neglect other aspects of our lives, which can negatively impact us not only physically, but also emotionally and socially (Sussman, 2012). This is because it means we neglect spending time on our well-being, spending time socialising with family or friends, making time for hobbies and so on. Thus, workaholism is said to be a type of "life imbalance" (Matuska, 2010).

I had never considered myself a "workaholic", partly due to a lack of awareness, and partly because for most of my career in my twenties (prior to my final job), I largely enjoyed my work. The many positives of my work outweighed the negatives, which perhaps was one of the reasons why, although I had "workaholic tendencies", I did not burnout before then. It has been suggested, for example, that burnout seems to be linked more with workaholics who experience low levels of job-related enjoyment, compared to other workaholics who experience higher levels of work-related enjoyment (McMillan & O'Driscoll, 2004).

Nevertheless, during the time between burnouts, I was recommended a book entitled Personality Adaptations by Joines and Stewart (2002). In this book, the authors identify six different personality adaptations, with "responsible-workaholic" being one of them. When I read their description of the "responsible-workaholic", I thought that is me to a tee! (*Although written for psychotherapists and counsellors, I highly recommend this book for further information on this.*)

For the first time, I became consciously aware that I have what I describe as "workaholic tendencies". It is not a surprise to me now, given my family history, their strong work ethic, with an emphasis on work rather than education (as my story demonstrates). I also relate to some of the research into workaholism and personality. Some researchers have found, for example, that people addicted to work are often what is described as "Type A" personality types, that is they are highly achievement-focused, driven to achieve, and perfectionists, who have difficulty delegating (Clark et al., 2016). Similarly, others have reported that there is a tendency for people who are addicted to work to refuse to accept that they are constantly tired and continue to push themselves beyond their limits, until physical ill-health prevents them from continuing to work, which results in them finally getting help (McMillan & O'Driscoll, 2004).

Becoming consciously aware of these aspects of myself has been helpful for me in relation to my burnout recovery, and concerning relapse prevention, as mentioned. Furthermore, this was also the case for some of the participants in the research into burnout recovery, those who reported becoming aware of their striving for perfection, and not delegating – which was an important aspect of their recovery – and for one participant whose whole journey was summed up as going from workaholism to balance (see Research Box).

Research Box:
In terms of the support for the benefit of self-awareness with regard to general well-being, Cowden and Meyer-Weitz's (2016) study into competitive tennis found that self-awareness, especially insight into the self, was important with regard to reducing stress and improving resilience in the participants. Additionally, Haugstvedt et al. (2011) researched self-awareness in relation to the process of returning to work in general. Their study investigated a counselling intervention that was based on Gestalt theory, like my first therapy experience, and mindfulness. Themes reported by their participants as important in their recovery process included raised awareness of their thoughts, emotions and signals from their bodies.

There is much less research into burnout recovery compared to prevention of burnout, as mentioned. However, of the research I have found, awareness has been identified as one of the main important factors consistently reported in the recovery process research (Andreou, 2015). An example is the study by Abedini et al. (2018) into burnout recovery among internal medicine residents, with some reporting that becoming aware that burnout was the cause of the symptoms they had been experiencing was a key aspect of their recovery.

Similarly, Salminen et al. (2015) investigated experiences of recovery during burnout rehabilitation and found that awareness was a key motivational factor in the change and recovery process for the participants. This included becoming aware of their own limitations and needs, in addition to which aspects of their personalities were implicated in their burnout development, including perfectionistic striving and problems with task delegation, for example (Salminen et al., 2015).

In the study by Andreou (2015), one of the participants' journey of recovery was described as going "from workaholism to finding balance", which included an increase in awareness. Furthermore, Fjellman-Wiklund et al. (2010) reported that "get to know myself" was a key theme in the recovery process for their participants, which included finding out what part, and how, they had in developing burnout. Finally, Regedanz (2008) described the process of reflecting, which included the participants learning about their values, as an important part of the recovery process for the participants in her study on job-related burnout.

Tips for raising awareness:
To raise awareness, I have found a number of strategies particularly helpful, some of which have already been mentioned, which are included here (please note this is not an exhaustive list):

- Make time for reflection and self-enquiry
- Seek professional support (psychotherapy, counselling, coaching, for example – depending on your personal history and your needs)
- Practising mindfulness in general, or doing specific mindful practices (e.g. mindful walking, mindful body scan etc.)
- Spending time sitting, meditating
- Reflecting and journaling – about your job, your challenges, health issues (the symptoms), relating to your burnout experiences
- Writing your story
- Attending a retreat
- Attending a self-development workshop
- Practise yoga, tai chi or qi gong, for example.

KEY TWO: RESTORE YOUR BODY

Take care of your body. It's the only place you have to live.
Jim Rohn

How we ignore our body and what it may be trying to tell us
Both my experiences of burnout were preceded by periods of chronic stress and it is now well established that chronic stress has negative health consequences, affecting our bodies in many ways. Additionally, exhaustion is one of the main significant features of burnout, and this too has been linked to stress-related health issues including immune-related issues, such as colds and flu, problems with sleep, along with "headaches, chronic fatigue, gastrointestinal disorders and muscle tension" (Maslach & Leiter, 2016).

I personally experienced many of the aforementioned physical health issues myself, in connection with the periods of chronic stress prior to burnout, particularly before the first burnout. I had an episode of the flu, digestive problems, mysterious pains in my limbs and increasing tiredness which eventually resulted in total exhaustion. With regard to the second burnout, I experienced exhaustion and I also experienced a period of weight gain, for the first time in my life.

Others have also reported experiencing bodily symptoms in relation to burnout, including heart problems, issues concerning blood pressure and problems with breathing or sleep and often no biological medically related cause is found for them (Arman et al., 2011). In addition, before burning out, some people have experienced frequent infection, pain and extreme fatigue and yet the individuals ignored these symptoms or overruled them (Ekstedt & Fagerberg, 2005). Therefore, what we also have in common is that we ignored, or denied, these symptoms and carried on pushing ourselves, until we could no longer. There is a great line in the film American Beauty: "never underestimate the power of denial", which I think reflects the process of ignoring or overriding our body's signals, particularly when they become so "loud".

At the time I was experiencing these symptoms (in relation to the first burnout), I perceived them as an often-uncomfortable inconvenience, hence the denial, and even more than that, especially in relation to the flu, they increased my anxiety. Firstly, I became anxious any time I had to take time off work, as it meant the workload would increase even further, so I would have even more to do when I returned (therefore, I did not take adequate time off to recuperate from the flu). Secondly, the longer the symptoms lasted and the worse they got, the more I became anxious as to what was actually wrong with me – and how it was impacting my ability to do my job. I was unsure how much longer I could continue.

Before I experienced the first burnout, my relationship with my body back then was like it was a different country, separate from my mind, like the UK and France pre the Eurotunnel! My mind was "the UK", the place where I "resided", the place where I was a "native speaker of the language". I knew the "cultural norms", the "rules and regulations" and I respected them. Being "in my mind" was my "comfort zone". It was "self-governing" and dominated and ruled "my world". In contrast, my body was something I rarely thought about (unless I was ill) or paid much attention to. It was like "France", a place that I "visited" occasionally, when I wanted a break. My "French" was basic, and I could get my basic needs met (food, drink, sex, "getting about" from A to B for example). But that was about it. It held minimal value for me then and if I had any issues, I would if necessary, seek help from others, like a "translator" (i.e. the GP).

Therefore, I was unaware at that time that the symptoms I was experiencing were my body's way of signalling to me that something was wrong, and that I needed to take action to address the problems, the work-related stress in particular. I did not realise at that time that my body was trying to tell me it could not be sustained by the food and drink I was consuming (a lot of pasta, sugar-laden products, snacks, chocolate, cake, coffee, tea, wine and minimal fruit and vegetables), or that worse, these things were having a negative impact on it. I had no idea that my body was trying to tell me that it was not a robot, and thus it could not maintain that level of output of activity, or that level of stress (not without the proper sustenance etc.) and that it needed to be "recharged" and have more of a balance.

Consequently, the greater my workload and the more stress I experienced, the more I neglected my body and its needs. I allowed the dictates of my mind to dominate my actions, which led me to push myself beyond my limits, beyond what was appropriate for my body, until I was forced to take action. One of the most frightening things I experienced in my first burnout was having the thoughts about moving, but my body not responding to these commands of my mind, for the first time ever in my life. It was a terrifying experience. This level of fear was a key motivational factor for me in taking control of my well-being and being committed to restoring my body, my health.

Listening to our body and meeting its needs
One of the first measures we need to take with regard to restoring the body is to pause and stop ignoring or overruling symptoms, and instead be willing to listen to our body and what it may be signalling to us. Although I referred to my body and mind as feeling like separate countries prior to the first burnout, and previously, it was believed that the mind had no influence on the body (i.e. Descartes' theory of Dualism), but of course they are interconnected. Furthermore, it is now well established that the mind impacts the body. Therefore, the focus of this key is on restoring the body but, by doing so, we are of course helping our mental, and emotional, well-being too, due to their interconnected relationship.

Obviously, we are all unique with differing constitutions, needs, tolerance and resilience levels and so on. Equally, the level of burnout people experience can vary too, from low levels to more severe levels of burnout. Consequently, I have only included a brief overview here of three areas that we need to attend to in order to restore our body as part of the burnout recovery process, namely nutrition, rest and relaxation, and physical activity (with the focus on exercise in particular). However, it is down to each individual to discover what their body needs and what is appropriate for them.

The good news is that addressing our physical needs can be one of the easiest aspects to address regarding action and burnout recovery. This is because it is often easier to raise our awareness of our bodies, than it is our minds and emotions, as how we treat ourselves physically is observable, once we stop and pay attention! We can actually see and monitor what food and drink we consume. It is easy to know what we do to rest and relax, if anything at all. It is easy to know if we belong to a gym and how regularly we visit it and what exercise we do whilst we are there. As I mentioned in the introduction, when we are trying to recover from severe burnout it is often helpful to start with what seems to be the easiest aspect.

The importance of good nutrition

Even in the 1980s, as part of helping healthcare professionals to avoid burnout, individuals were advised to have "good nutrition" (Leigthon & Roye, 1984). However, when I experienced my first burnout, it was still many years before the obesity and diabetes crises and so, a lot less attention was paid to nutrition back then. Thankfully, times have changed. We have become much more aware of the importance of nutrition for our health and well-being, not only physically but also in relation to our mental well-being. There is, for example, even a field of research, known as "nutritional psychiatry", and this area of research has found evidence to support the link between our diet and our mental health (Karr, 2019).

Although there is still much confusion concerning what is the best diet for weight loss, there is general agreement about what constitutes good nutrition. We now know that we need to eat lots of fresh fruit and vegetables, with the promotion of the "five-a-day" campaign, for example. We know that it also includes a "balanced diet", meaning a variety of food, with the emphasis still on fresh fruit and vegetables, and that the Mediterranean diet is widely considered to offer this, and perceived as healthy (see Research Box). We have even become aware of the benefits of certain vitamins and minerals, with many of us increasingly supplementing our diet to boost our nutritional intake. Additionally, we are now very aware of the dangers of consuming too much sugar, processed food and red meat, for example.

Aside from the basics of good nutrition, it is up to each individual to know what their body needs, what is right for them to consume, particularly with the increase of allergies and sensitivities. Although it can feel overwhelming at times, I found reading about nutrition helpful during my recovery process and I found The Optimum Nutrition Bible by Patrick Holford, along with other books, really useful. Furthermore, if we have the means to do so, it can be even more helpful to seek the advice of a qualified nutritionist (see Resources). Keeping a record of what we consume on a daily basis is a useful start to address the nutrition aspect, as it increases our awareness of where we may be doing well, and where we may be lacking, nutritionally.

Once we have the awareness of what we need, we need to make the commitment to give that to ourselves, not only in regard to nutrition, but also rest and relaxation, and physical activity, which can be challenging. Therefore, it can be useful to remember that the more we restore our body, through good nutrition and so on, the more we can regain our energy, our resilience and thus, the more we will gain our lives back.

Why adequate rest and relaxation are essential

Our bodies are amazing really. They have a perfect design, including an innate system to help us to recover, namely the "rest and repair" system, also known as the parasympathetic nervous system (PNS). The challenge we can experience is that when we are chronically stressed, the "fight/flight/freeze" system, otherwise known as the sympathetic nervous system (SNS) is activated and for too long. Hence, in order to repair ourselves, we need to activate the PNS instead (for a detailed description of this process, and the effects of chronic stress on the body, see www.thecompassiondoctor.com).

Additionally, physical tension in the body is associated with stress. It is a part of the SNS response. It was designed to enable us to do what we needed to do to physically survive when we were faced with a physical threat. Therefore, if we do not make efforts to regularly de-stress and release tension, it builds up, so that with chronic stress we can experience chronic tension, as in the case of burnout. We can then find that we have had this level of tension for so long that we are not even consciously aware that we are holding tension, as I personally experienced. Thus, one of the strategies to help restore the body is to become consciously aware of where, and when, we are holding tension in the body. Mindfulness, that is, taking a moment at regular intervals throughout the day (or at least at the beginning, middle and end of the day) to notice any tension in our body, is a useful tool for this. Some of the areas we most commonly hold tension in are our shoulders, our head (especially in the temples and jaw) and our stomachs.

Following awareness, there are some other techniques to actively release tension and relax. Time off from work, resting and catching up on sleep are important factors of the recovery process (see Research Box) and restoring our body. However, in order to enhance PNS activation, other measures are also helpful. Relaxation techniques, such as Shultz's "Autogenic Training" or Benson's (2000) "Relaxation Response", where we intentionally relax our muscles, can be used. We can also practise meditation or do a course in Mindfulness-based Stress Reduction (MBSR), for example, which are practices whereby we do not set out to intentionally relax, but it occurs as a result of the practices to varying degrees.

Relaxation techniques have also been reported in burnout recovery literature as helpful to the process (see Research Box). Additionally, many people find that doing physical exercise helps them to relax, which although this is not restful at the time, it may result in a period of enhanced rest afterwards, such as through deeper sleep.

Holistic health treatments are another way to help the body to relax, including massage, reflexology, acupressure, shiatsu and so on. These are very helpful if we are feeling exhausted but have the funds to pay for treatments. Alternatively, we can do some of them on ourselves if we lack the funds, such as massaging the parts of our bodies that we can reach (feet and hands etc.). However, what one person finds relaxing, another may find irritating or actually stress-inducing or anxiety-provoking. Therefore, as with all of these aspects, it is important that we find what works for us, experimenting if we need to, until we identify what that is.

The importance of physical activity for health and well-being
The benefits of physical activity are also well established. The WHO (2020) reported that physical activity has significant health benefits for our bodies (as well as our hearts and minds), and improves our overall well-being, for example. Exercise is a physical activity that when practiced regularly enhances our ability to cope with stress and improves our sleep (Karr, 2019). Similarly, as part of avoiding burnout, in addition to good nutrition mentioned previously, healthcare professionals have been advised to exercise regularly (Leighton & Roye, 1984). Another benefit of physical activity in general, is that it helps us to relax and thus release tension, which is an important aspect of burnout recovery, as discussed. There are some reports in the burnout recovery literature too, of physical activity (especially regular exercise) being helpful to the process of recovery (see Research Box).

The questions people may have include, what type of physical activity, particularly in regard to exercise, is best for burnout recovery, how often do we need to do it and how long for? This is not something that I have found covered in the research. Again, as with the nutrition aspect, it depends on the extent to which we feel burnt out, the level of exhaustion, our age, our general fitness levels and so on, and it is best to seek the advice of a qualified professional, if possible. Alternatively, we can explore what we might like to do and attempt that, or perhaps return to a physical exercise that we used to enjoy and found beneficial in the past, but that we have neglected, or not been able to do for whatever reason.

My first burnout recovery

I think, in hindsight, I would say that the measures I initially took to restore my body the first time, was to accept that I could not push my body any further and resign from work. I really was then "forced" to rest as I was too exhausted to do anything else at first. I would now liken the rest of the journey of restoring my body, using the metaphor previously mentioned, like "building the Channel Tunnel" between my mind and my body, as it involved "excavating" – eliminating what was in the way of recovery – and "building" a new "tunnel" of communication. There were many "workers" who helped with the "project", and new unexpected discoveries made along the way, as I described previously:

> [I explored] alternative treatments including acupuncture and kinesiology. It also motivated me to seek advice from a qualified naturopath and nutritionist, who suggested I had some blood tests...I discovered I had [it was suggested] Candida Albicans (a yeast overgrowth) and several food intolerances...the naturopath designed a special diet for me which involved excluding gluten, wheat, sugar, dairy, yeast, caffeine and a few other products. (Buchan, 2008; pg. 78)

Although most of the alternative, or holistic, health treatments made me feel more relaxed and also eased some of the muscle pain I had been experiencing, it was the change in diet that helped make a dramatic difference to my symptoms and increased my energy levels, as I explain in my story, in Part Two. Additionally, it was helpful to learn about the effects of certain foods on the body, such as sugar and caffeine for example, and how they stimulate the SNS, triggering the release of adrenaline. This is detrimental to the body when it needs to be in the "rest and repair" mode, which requires the PNS to be activated, as previously mentioned. This knowledge, and how I was feeling as a result, helped me to continue on the diet for about two years or more.

After which time, when I felt fully recovered, I began to experiment with re-introducing some things into my diet, with the exception of gluten (as around the time of the burnout I was also diagnosed with coeliac disease). However, I still generally maintained a healthy, balanced diet after that, with minimal processed foods or sugar and caffeine (except for brief periods, such as holidays abroad, my birthday or Christmas), because my body felt so much better when I stuck to it and I placed a high value on maintaining my well-being.

I also discovered meditation as part of my recovery, taught myself how to do it and began a regular practice, as mentioned previously. I found it helped me relax mentally and physically. I found out about the concept of what is referred to in meditation as "grounding", that is, bringing our conscious awareness into our body, and particularly our feet. I found the grounding practice really useful for helping reduce my stress and anxiety.

Prior to burning out, I had neglected physical exercise. I was not motivated to exercise as I had so many other, what I considered more important tasks to fit into my day, especially work, and being blessed with a high metabolism and being a weight that remained at a constant level I was happy with, I felt it was never an issue. By the time I burnt out, I was so exhausted that physical activity, even the daily tasks of getting showered and dressed, was very difficult initially. When I felt able to, I went for gentle walks, gradually building up over time with longer walks. This was balanced with sufficient rest.

It took me about two and a half years to feel as though I had restored my body (and mind) and felt recovered. On reflection, I think it may have taken that long because although I did all of the above, as soon as I had some energy, and the more my energy increased, the more I slipped back into my old patterns. I let my mind (my driven, "type A" personality) dictate my decisions, rather than considering what would be the best choice for my body at that time, as is reflected in my story in Part Two, when I undertook other training courses, in addition to trying to complete my undergraduate degree. This pattern is also partly why I experienced the second burnout.

My second burnout recovery
Thankfully, I had some but fewer health-related issues in connection with my second experience of burnout and this time, I had all the knowledge gained from, and after, the first experience. Therefore, when I addressed this aspect of recovery, I had to accept that once again, I had been pushing my body too much for too long, and that I

needed to stop and take some time out. Hence, my decision to not pursue the process of getting my NHS contract renewed (as I explain in my story in Part Two).

I knew I had also not been sticking to good nutrition either, having again slipped back into the habit of prioritising work over this aspect of my self-care – and everything else! Consequently, once I stopped working, I addressed this as soon as I could. I saw another practitioner and I read even more about health, nutrition, the stress response, adrenal fatigue and so on. I experimented to see what worked best for me. In the end, I discovered what was most beneficial for me personally in regard to restoring my body was avoiding sugar, caffeine (even decaffeinated coffee and tea), chocolate, cacao, bread (even gluten-free bread), medium to high processed foods (e.g. ready meals, most packaged gluten-free products), alcohol and carbonated drinks. Cutting out red meat and eggs also seemed to help.

Additionally, I increased my intake of fresh fruit, vegetables, pulses, legumes, nuts and seeds, and water and herbal teas. At some point I had sessions with another nutritionist to try and speed up the process. She recommended a large variety of supplements. I took them for a few months. However, not only was it costing a fortune, I found the high expense and trying to remember when to take them all extremely stressful, which was then counter-productive! So, I stopped that. I reduced it to just green barley grass, a probiotic, vitamin C and vitamin D. I have found that this is also the best diet for me with regard to maintaining my health and well-being and preventing burnout relapse, which is why I stick to it as much as is practically possible.

Furthermore, I turned my attention to rest and relaxation, starting with getting some much-needed rest. I was also very consciously aware that I had not kept up with my mindfulness practice, dropping it as the workload and stress increased prior to burnout, even though I knew how much I personally benefited from it. Again, it was another example of prioritising work over self-care. After some initial resistance (as I explain in Part Two), I returned to a regular mindfulness practice once more as part of restoring my body, mind and soul.

Another difference with the second burnout recovery was that, as I experienced fewer health-related conditions, and had much greater knowledge regarding recovery and well-being by then, I was

27

motivated to include exercise as part of restoring my body. I did Hatha yoga and regularly walked my dog, pacing myself, building up my stamina and strength again, over time. Consequently, even though I was quite a bit older when I experienced the second burnout, because I had gained the knowledge and skills that I have, and implemented the changes described, it did not impair my recovery. Furthermore, I perceive that I am stronger and have more stamina now than I had when I recovered from the first burnout.

Research Box:

General points
The participants in the Salminen et al. (2015) study made efforts to have more balance in their life, in addition to being more sensitive to their bodies' signals, which were reported as important aspects of their burnout recovery process. Similarly, individuals in the investigation by Fjellman-Wiklund et al. (2010) found that the recovery process included utilising the signals from their bodies to increase their self-awareness and establish appropriate limits. Restoring one's health was the third stage in the recovery process (after the stages of admitting the problem and distancing from work) reported in Bernier's (1998) study into recovery from burnout and other reactions to severe work-related stress.

Rest and relaxation
Regular mindfulness meditation practice has been found to help to decrease burnout symptoms in physicians, as it reduces stress and improves both physical and emotional well-being (Karr, 2019). In the research by Abedini et al. (2018), internal medicine residents reported that time off work helped their recovery, and this time off for some individuals included making sleep a priority.

Relaxing during leisure time has been found to decrease burnout and enhance well-being for those working with cancer patients (Poulsen et al., 2015). Similarly, Oerlemans and Bakker (2014), who investigated burnout and daily recovery, found that people experiencing high levels of burnout need to stop any work-related activity after work and instead spend time on activities which require little effort, such as resting or not doing anything at all (Oerlemans & Bakker, 2014).

The rehabilitation programme for burnout recovery referred to in the study by Hätinen et al. (2013) included health education and group discussions on a variety of topics including relaxation. The significance of rest and relaxation in the burnout recovery process was also reported by some participants of another burnout rehabilitation programme, who reported becoming aware of how important it was to make time for rest and relaxation (Fjellman-Wiklund et al., 2010). Furthermore, part of the recovery process for those in the Arman et al. (2011) study included finding

28

a new relation, in other words more of a balance, between doing activities and resting.

Nutrition

Neves, Amorim and Salomon (2020) reviewed the research into burnout in teachers and the relationship with nutrition. They found evidence suggesting a positive link between good nutrition and better mental health, concluding that good nutrition can be helpful for both preventing and treating burnout in teachers.

Likewise, Esquivel (2020) recommended the development of nutrition strategies, albeit for reducing the risk of burnout, in physicians and other healthcare workers, and given the research evidence, is in favour of these workers adopting the Mediterranean diet, in addition to other strategies, including eating mindfully. Similarly, Hamidi, Boggild and Cheung (2016) investigated burnout in physicians and reported that sufficient nutrition, along with adequate hydration, are important with regard to maintaining health and well-being.

Salminen et al. (2015) researched the experiences of those attending a burnout rehabilitation programme, as mentioned previously. The programme, which aimed to help people recover from burnout, included a variety of individual and group-based interventions, including health education, which encompassed education regarding nutrition.

Physical activity

Gerber et al. (2020) found that individuals with greater levels of physical activity reported fewer symptoms of burnout at stressful times, for example, and consequently, they suggest regular physical activity in non-work time can help employees to feel more equipped to manage work-related stress. Poulsen et al. (2015) also reported that doing what they describe as "strenuous physical activity" was related to "high recovery" from burnout in the participants in their study.

For those in the Salminen et al. (2015) investigation into a burnout rehabilitation programme, individuals made efforts to having more balance in their life, which included incorporating physical exercise. Likewise, in their study into a rehabilitation programme which included qi gong exercises, encompassing a combination of movements, breathing and meditation, participants reported these activities helped them to experience relaxation (physically and mentally) and what they described as a "positive tiredness" (Fjellman-Wiklund et al., 2010). Similarly, the rehabilitation programme for burnout recovery referred to in the study by Hätinen et al. (2013) also included physical exercise.

Oerlemans and Bakker (2014) investigated daily recovery from burnout. As part of their study, they assessed the time spent by participants in their non-work time on non-work-related activities. This included physical activities, which ranged from tennis, hockey and swimming to dancing and fitness, for example. The researchers reported non-significant results for the effects of physical activity on the daily recovery from burnout for the participants in their study, which they consider might be because for people high in burnout, physical activity might increase physical tiredness, which might counteract its positive benefits.

Tips for restoring your body:
Please see your GP if you are experiencing any health issue.
However, I include the following tips as I found them helpful in restoring my body following burnout:

- Address nutrition. Keep a diary for a typical week and record all the food and drink consumed. Make an assessment. How healthy is your diet? How balanced is it? Are you well hydrated or do you need to drink more water? What changes do you need to make given what you have read and any other knowledge you may have about this? If you are unsure, and have the financial means, seek support from a qualified nutritionist or naturopath (see Resources).
- Address the need for rest. Seek help and support (ask family members etc. to help out if possible, even for a short while, especially if you have dependants that need taking care of) if you need to, so that you can get some rest.
- Take action regarding relaxation. Identify what helps you to genuinely feel relaxed. Schedule in regular relaxation – whether that is through mindfulness practice or holistic health treatments (either with a practitioner or doing them on yourself).
- Become consciously aware of the tension in your body and your breathing, by checking at points in the day. You could take a mindful minute right now for example, to notice your breathing. How is it? Is it short, sharp and shallow, from your chest, or deep and relaxed, from your belly? Is there any tension in your body? If so where?
- Address physical activity, particularly exercise. Given what you know about yourself, your body, your level of burnout, consider whether you are doing enough, or the right type, of physical activity that your body may require in order to feel restored. If it is more a question of motivation, you may like to experiment with a range of physical activities, including

30

sport and exercise, if appropriate for you, to find something that you would feel more motivated to do. Is there an activity you used to find beneficial and enjoyable but have neglected, or not been able to do for a while? Could you return to that? It can also be useful, if you have the means, to seek the advice of a qualified personal trainer or someone qualified in the physical activity that you are considering (as I did with yoga, for example).

- Most importantly – with all of this – listen to your body. Give it some time and quality attention, give it what it needs, to help it do what it is naturally designed to do, (given the right conditions) – and restore itself.

KEY THREE: BE TRUE TO YOURSELF

*To be yourself in a world that is constantly trying to make you
something else is the greatest accomplishment.*
Ralph Waldo Emerson

What does it mean to be true to yourself?

Being true to ourselves involves authenticity. Definitions of authenticity are varied and can change, depending on the context (Hicks, Schlegel & Newman, 2019). For the sake of simplicity, when I refer to authenticity in this key, I am referring to "the quality of being real or true" (The Cambridge Dictionary, 2020). An aspect of being true to ourselves was covered in the first key, namely becoming aware of our thoughts, feelings, needs, wants and so on. Additionally, being true to ourselves means we stop ignoring or overruling any physical symptoms, or pushing ourselves excessively, or neglecting the needs of our body, and instead attend to our physical selves and its needs properly, as discussed in the second key.

However, being true to ourselves also involves becoming aware of (or revisiting) what gives us meaning in our lives, by identifying our values, in addition to living those values, which is what this key focuses on. Another concept associated with being authentic is autonomy. Autonomy means "the ability to make your own decisions without being controlled by anyone else" (The Cambridge Dictionary, 2020). In order to be able to live our values, and other aspects of authenticity, a certain level of assertiveness and the ability to set boundaries is required, which is what the remainder of this key focuses on.

It is important to perceive authenticity, and autonomy as being on a continuum, rather than absolutes. It is vital for our well-being to be completely authentic with ourselves, such that we acknowledge to ourselves our thoughts and feelings, rather than suppress or deny them, for example. Nevertheless, being authentic is a process that involves skill and courage (Schlegel, Hicks, King & Arndt, 2011). Thus, being authentic with anyone else requires a level of discernment, as it depends on the context and the potential consequences of being authentic, in addition to our level of skill and courage.

This is particularly the case in relation to our working lives, referred to in psychology as "authenticity at work" (Van den Bosch & Taris, 2014a) (see Research Box for further information on this). Sometimes the benefits of being true to ourselves at work may be outweighed by the negatives (Zhang et al., 2019). Additionally, being true to ourselves may mean that we actually have to leave our job, or even our career, as in my case. Therefore, with regard to work-related authenticity, we need to take into consideration many aspects, including the level of psychological safety, potential consequences and so on, when discerning how authentic it is appropriate for us to be at work, for example, in addition to how skilled we are, and how courageous, in this area.

Similarly, with regard to autonomy, whilst it is beneficial for our well-being to be independent and resist pressure from others to behave in certain ways, we are social beings. Cooperating and collaborating with others is what has helped us survive and thrive (Baumeister, 2019). Thus, although being true to ourselves involves a certain level of autonomy, it needs to be at a level that is appropriate, especially at work, such that it still enables us to work in collaboration with others. In summary, being true to ourselves, particularly in regard to other people and generally in our society today, is challenging and takes courage. Due to the challenges associated with it, being true to ourselves is therefore considered to be an "everyday achievement" for each person (Ryan & Ryan, 2019).

Why being true to yourself is important
If being true to ourselves is so challenging, we may naturally want to know, why would we even try to do it, or learn and develop assertiveness skills, especially given our busy lives or how exhausted we may feel? There are negative consequences to being inauthentic both in our personal lives and at work. With regard to authenticity in the work context, the person–environment (P–E) fit, which means how compatible the person is with their work environment – good P–E fit, is when both are "well matched" (Kristof-Brown et al., 2005) – is important. This encompasses both the job itself and the organisation we work in and its values. We can liken the P–E fit to dating and our compatibility with a partner. Although the subject of P–E fit is a large one, I refer to it here only briefly, and because it was linked to both my experiences of burnout (see below). There are

negative consequences when there is not a good P–E fit. A mismatch has been linked to stress, for example (Edwards, Caplan & Harrison, 1998). Furthermore, the larger the misfit between the person and their work environment, the lower the level of well-being (Van den Bosch et al., 2019).

A link between a lack of authenticity at work and burnout has also been found. Those who experience lower levels of authenticity have been found to experience feeling alienated and disconnected from their true self at work, and this tends to be linked to increased burnout levels (Van den Bosch and Taris, 2014b). Similarly, not being true to ourselves means we avoid facing our challenging thoughts, feelings or actions, for example, which is also problematic. This is because, as I wrote previously, "negative thoughts, feelings and behaviours take a great deal of effort to [suppress] or cope with. ... They are energy draining and tension-inducing" (Buchan, 2008). This creates stress, and if this continues and becomes chronic, it can result in negative health consequences. Additionally, an important aspect of being true to ourselves means not just reading through this book, but also committing to take control of our recovery and implement any action necessary. This includes listening to our body's signals because "our body tells us when we are not being true to ourselves, if we pay attention to its signals" (Buchan, 2008).

Therefore, the main reason for being true to ourselves is that it is important for our physical and mental well-being. Gandhi described happiness as "when what you think, what you say and what you do are in harmony", which is what being our true authentic selves means. Autonomy is a characteristic of authenticity, as previously mentioned, and it is also significant. It is another one of the six characteristics considered to be important for psychological well-being (Ryff, 1995). This psychological need, being fundamental, must be met if we are to flourish and experience well-being (Ryan & Ryan, 2019). Other factors reflecting the importance of being true to ourselves are also described in the subsequent sections, specifically, those concerning finding meaning, assertiveness and boundary setting.

Find meaning
Having meaning in life is a fundamental part of being human. It is important for our well-being and a significant aspect of being true to ourselves. It is another of Ryff's (1989/1995) six concepts necessary for psychological well-being, for example, within the category of

"purpose in life", described as having a sense of direction, goals and a feeling life has meaning and purpose. Thus, a lack of meaning in life is linked to a number of health issues, including depression, for example (Martela & Pessi, 2018). Additionally, there is a link between burnout and meaningfulness, with a theory being that burnout is not only about working excessively, but that it also arises from a lack of meaning (along with a lack of joy) (Strümpfer, 2003). This has been described as an existential explanation of burnout (e.g. Arman et al., 2011). Hence, we need meaning in our lives to be resilient and to thrive (Strümpfer, 2003) and therefore, it is an important aspect of burnout recovery (see Research Box).

In order to discover what gives us meaning, if we are unaware of this, we can start by identifying our core values, that is, what is most important to us, and then making those a priority. To be true to ourselves, we then need to take action to actually live the values that we hold dear to us. This is the challenging part of meaning and being true to ourselves because it is one thing to become aware of what our core values are, and it is another to ensure that we live those values, particularly if we have a conflict of values, which is common.

We can find meaning in any area of life. Traditionally, we often found meaning in religion, but this has declined over the years, and we more frequently obtain meaning in our work (or from our family) (Baumeister, 1991). I found meaning in my work for many years. In my first career, the work I was doing was aligned with my values for a long time, that is, I experienced a good P–E fit (referred to previously) for most of it. Then something changed and the work especially began to lack meaning for me, which was further compounded by the poor P–E fit in my final role. Although I took action to find meaning in my life by applying to retrain in psychology, it still meant having to endure many months in the job until I would start the new course. Consequently, I was still not being true to myself in so many areas, which eventually resulted in the first burnout.

With regard to the second burnout I experienced, it was a bit more complex than the first situation. By then, I knew that I derived meaning from helping people change and improve their lives. I was aware it was important to me to work for the NHS full time. It is the main reason I spent the money, time and effort that I did on doing the doctorate, training to be a counselling psychologist. However, by then I also knew that my well-being was still important to me. The extra complication was that there had been changes in the NHS (budget cuts etc.). Its values had changed in many ways, some of which I explain in my story. This included valuing Cognitive Behavioural Therapy (CBT) above all other therapies (there are approximately 450 psychological therapies!), for numerous reasons. Although the doctorate I did included some training in CBT, it was minimal.

Furthermore, for reasons that are beyond the scope of this book, CBT may be aligned with some of my values (the mind-related ones), but it is not aligned with my core, heart-felt values. Thus, on reflection, I can now see that I stopped being true to myself when I accepted the job in the NHS. This is because it included intense training in CBT, along with only being permitted to deliver this form of therapy to clients, even when it was not the most appropriate therapy for a particular client. I found it so challenging to experience the lack of alignment with my values as a humanistic practitioner who tailors solutions to each client's particular needs with regard to the client work aspect.

Additionally, particularly after four years of studying, it was incredibly difficult when I was already feeling tired, to then be trying to cram my mind with knowledge of all these "manualised" therapies for each of the different issues, which again, clashed with my core values. It really felt like my soul was being slowly destroyed. It is no wonder then, that I experienced the second burnout, especially because burnout has been described as a representation of "an erosion of the human soul" (Maslach & Leiter, 1997; cited in Strümpfer, 2003). Moreover, I neglected to be true to myself when I ignored the signals from my body, which started early on in the job, that this was not right for me. Therefore, as I mentioned previously, finding meaning is not only about being aware of our core values, it is even more important to then take action to live these values. Consequently, my recovery involved both of these aspects.

The importance of practising assertiveness and setting boundaries

Another important part of being authentic is being assertive. Being assertive means to be "confident and direct in claiming one's rights or putting forward one's views" (Collins English Dictionary, 2020). Hence, assertiveness involves standing up for ourselves, expressing our thoughts, feelings and needs and setting boundaries. It involves saying no when we need to, to respect our boundaries. Moreover, the use of assertiveness has evolved over the years, from initially being used in clinical practice as a strategy to aid mental health problems, then as a method of protecting human rights, followed by it being used as a self-development strategy and finally, as an important part of business communication skills (Peneva & Mavrodiev, 2013).

Furthermore, assertiveness has been described as a "balancing act" (Ames et al., 2017) which I think is very apt. It perfectly describes the challenge of asserting ourselves enough so that we meet our needs and support our well-being, but not too much, or ineffectively, so that it is detrimental to our interpersonal relationships. Equally, asserting ourselves appropriately means we need to avoid abusing others' rights too (Peneva & Mavrodiev, 2013). Assertiveness is therefore best perceived as a continuum, with excessive agreeableness, i.e. "unassertive" or "submissive" at one end, and excessive hostility, i.e. "aggressive", at the other end, with both extremes being problematic (Speed, Goldstein & Goldfried, 2018). Thus, we need to aim for a level of assertiveness that is somewhere between these two extreme ends of the spectrum.

This is also important to remember of course, not only regarding our personal relationships, but especially in the context of work. We may need to consider this with regard to working in collaboration and cooperatively, for example, and also in other situations within the context of work when our needs may differ from the needs of the organisation. We can find that what we perceive as our roles and responsibilities are different to what the organisation perceives or expects from us. This ambiguity, or mismatch, often causes stress, particularly as it blurs the boundaries of what is expected of us as employees (as I explain in my story). Therefore, in such a situation, we need to practise assertiveness so that the roles and responsibilities are clarified, and the ambiguity thus resolved. We are then subsequently more equipped to assert our boundaries.

This aspect of being true to ourselves, that is, issues with assertiveness, such as setting boundaries, has also been implicated with regard to burnout, as I personally experienced in relation to my first burnout experience, as demonstrated in my story. It started with me not pursuing clarity with regard to my role and responsibilities once I began working for the organisation, which contributed to my inability to set appropriate boundaries. This, in addition to the tendency I had to avoid conflict and be overly accommodating, meant that as my workload became excessive, I felt powerless to take action to remedy the situation. Similarly, although I did have a high level of autonomy, it was too much for me in that context, and, because of my lack of assertiveness, I felt unable to balance this amount of autonomy with requesting the support I actually needed. Others have also reported that addressing these aspects has been important with regard to their experiences of burnout recovery (see Research Box).

My first burnout recovery
I had no real idea about the concept of authenticity – being true to yourself – prior to the first burnout. I was also unaware that meaning in life was an important aspect of psychological well-being, but I knew I wanted more meaning in my life, which is why I had the goal to change careers. However, once I resigned from my job due to the burnout, I had months before I started re-training. Consequently, until I could derive meaning from a new career, I found meaning and purpose in having the goal of trying to become well enough to start the degree in psychology and counselling.

Additionally, part of my recovery process involved learning to find meaning in other things, aside from a career, in order to improve my well-being. This included personal growth (therapy, self-help and so on), along with attending a short course in musical theatre, something I had longed to do but had not had the courage to do previously. When my energy improved, I also became a volunteer with an organisation called Alternatives (see Resources), as volunteering is a well-established method of finding meaning in life.

Although the first step on my burnout recovery was resigning from my job, and thus the assertiveness and boundary issue in that context was resolved, I knew there was another way of "being", of behaving in the world, especially at work, because I had observed other people who I considered to be assertive and able to stand up for themselves. However, I did not know how to change and become like that myself. Thus, it was one of the first aspects of my burnout recovery that I asked my therapist to help me with.

My therapist explained the difference between authentically being assertive, expressing my thoughts and feelings and so on (when appropriate) and in contrast to using manipulation (overtly or covertly) to get one's needs met. She taught me the importance of "owning" my thoughts, feelings, needs and so on, by using "I" statements, as part of practising assertiveness (in addition to increasing authenticity). Therapy was also useful for role-playing, which helped me develop my assertiveness skills further, within a psychologically safe environment.

In between sessions, as with the other keys to recovery, I continued to read self-help books when I had the energy. I found the chapter on teaching other people how to treat you in a book called Pulling Your Own Strings (Dyer, 1997), particularly helpful at that time. I also followed the suggestion of Whitefield (1987) and created my own personal "bill of rights". A significant "right" for me included the right to say no, along with the right to have my needs and wants respected by others. I found having this personal "bill of rights", along with the therapy, transformational. To have this clear idea of what I would and would not accept was like a compass for me, in terms of directing my assertive behaviour – in conjunction with my values.

Because learning assertiveness is a skill developed through knowledge and practice, I found it helpful (and appropriate) to start with practising within the safe context of therapy, as mentioned. I was living back home with my family and so I was able to, and needed to, practise my new skills with them too. Initially, it was challenging as it created arguments and conflict – which is to be expected and normal when we start to behave differently with others. Nevertheless, thanks to having the support of the therapist, who was skilled in this area, I could verify with her whether I was "doing it right". I could check with her, if what I had said and how I had behaved was actually reasonable, and appropriate – because I had no idea at that time, as being true to myself was all so new to me.

I would say that learning to be true to myself, not only with regard to taking action to give myself heart-felt meaning in my life, in addition to developing my assertiveness skills, is another aspect of the metaphor I referred to in the second key, of "building the Channel Tunnel" between my head and my heart. It was not a straightforward process, but it was ultimately successful – for a number of years!

My second burnout recovery
In regard to my second burnout experience, I was very consciously aware of what being true to myself meant. I was very aware of my values, that is to say, I was aware of my value of deriving meaning from helping others change and improve their lives. However, the problem was I had not continued to be true to myself, my authentic self. Instead, I had allowed my dominant, driven mind to dictate my choice of job, and also to prioritise work over everything else once

more. I had allowed fear (of missing out on an opportunity etc.) to overrule my true feelings, which wanted to choose a very different path. It was as though the "Channel Tunnel" was blocked!

Consequently, in order to recover, I had to spend time reflecting on the ways in which I had stopped being true to myself and uncover what had led to that, so that I could learn the lessons and prevent another relapse. Furthermore, I had to forgive myself and practise self-acceptance and self-compassion (as I explain in the fourth key). I then re-visited my core values and made a commitment to myself that no matter how much my rational, logical mind might protest, I would take action to give that to myself. This resulted in me working with my husband and returning to my mindfulness practice, including undertaking training in it (including in compassion practices), something I had longed to do for years. I also did other things to "heal my soul" (explained further in the subsequent keys).

After years of personal development work, professional training in psychology, communication skills, coaching and so forth, practising assertiveness is no longer an issue. The only aspect of assertiveness that I needed to work on concerned being what I refer to as "internally assertive" with regard to my mind, so that I no longer allow it to dominate and dictate all my actions, and instead have more of a balance in my life between my head and my heart. What was, and continues to be, essential for this is practising mindfulness (and compassion) regularly along with other forms of meditation, ensuring I make time for the other aspects of my life, not just work. Scheduling in time off to rest and recharge after particularly intense (but short) periods of work or projects, helps with this, as I mention in Part Two.

Research Box:

General points
There is research which demonstrates that individuals who are more authentic in general experience better well-being (Ryan & Ryan, 2019). Authenticity is linked not only to greater individual well-being, but also to healthy relationships (Zhang et al., 2019). Furthermore, authenticity is also beneficial with regard to engagement with one's work (Sutton, 2020).

"Authenticity at work" is described as the degree to which an employee "feels in touch with their true self while at work" (Van den Bosch et al., 2019; pg. 247). Van den Bosch et al. (2014a) devised a way to measure authenticity at work according to three dimensions. These include "self-alienation" – when a person experiences a sense of feeling disconnected from their true self whilst at work; "authentic living" – the extent that a person is their authentic self at work, behaving in ways that are aligned with their values and beliefs and "accepting external influence" – the amount to which a person "accepts external influence of others" and considers they meet others' expectations (cited in Van den Bosch et al, 2019). According to Van den Bosch et al. (2014a) we experience the optimum amount of authenticity at work when we experience the following: low levels of self-alienation and low levels of acceptance of external influence and high levels of authentic living.

With regard to P–E fit, mentioned previously, this also includes the person–job fit, and the person–organisation fit too. Person–job fit relates to the suitability of the individual for the job they are employed to do. Person–organisation fit concerns the extent to which an individual's core values and beliefs are aligned with the organisation's values and culture (Chatman, 1989). With regard to burnout, Tong, Wang and Peng (2015) found that both person–job and person–organisation fit was associated with burnout.

Meaning
Finding meaning once again within the field of medicine itself, or from their relationships with their patients and colleagues, or in improving their knowledge and skills was reported by internal medicine residents in their burnout recovery (Abedini et al., 2018). Similarly, in their small study on burnout recovery, one of their four participants described how an essential part of their recovery included reprioritising their values (Salminen et al., 2017).

By the end of the rehabilitation programme the participants of the Salminen et al. (2015) investigation reported that they had subsequently found meaning in life, and some reported they had rediscovered meaning in their job. Likewise, some of the individuals in another study found meaning as a result of learning to find value in things other than in work-related aspects, with it no longer being important to obtain "the best job" (Fjellman-Wiklund et al., 2010) for example.

In their study investigating burnout as an "existential deficiency", mentioned previously, Arman et al. (2011), found that part of the recovery process included "experiencing the meaning of life and authenticity". Although investigating burnout from a different perspective, not as an existential deficiency, Regedanz (2008) also found that participants' job burnout recovery process included learning about values.

Moreover, in a study investigating successful recovery from severe burnout and other reactions to severe work-related stress, one of the stages of recovery reported by participants was a "questioning values" stage (Bernier, 1998). Finally, although investigating returning to work in general rather than following burnout specifically, strategies that were reported as being important to the recovery change process also included discussions about core values (Haugstvedt et al., 2011).

Assertiveness and boundaries
Research has found a relationship between assertiveness and burnout too. The internal medical residents in one study reported they believe what contributed to their burnout was a knowledge deficit regarding how to establish boundaries with patients because it meant that they then "overextended themselves" with regard to caring for them (Abendini et al., 2018). Consequently, developing assertiveness skills, including boundary setting, supported their recovery and enhanced their relapse prevention of burnout.

Similarly, some of the participants in the investigation into a rehabilitation programme found that "enhanced assertiveness" was linked to an increase in respect for themselves (Salminen et al., 2015). This, in turn, was associated with becoming more assertive at work, including being proactive in regard to making or requesting work-related changes.

An important aspect of the rehabilitation process investigated by Fjellman-Wiklund et al. (2010) meant that some individuals began altering how they decided their priorities and learning to set boundaries, which included using the body as a guide. They also reported learning the importance of resisting the expectations of others, which could be described as an increase in authenticity and autonomy. Finally, one of the many strategies employed by the individuals in the Regedanz (2008) study into job burnout recovery also included asserting boundaries.

Tips for being true to yourself:
Here are some tips, which I found helpful, regarding being true to myself and burnout recovery:

- Make some time to reflect honestly on your life. Identify the areas you perceive you are being true to yourself, or that you find it easy to do so, and areas you perceive you are struggling with this. Use this knowledge to make changes where you need to.
- Take the time to identify (or revisit) your core, heart-felt values in relation to work. Review the information about "authenticity at work" and "P−E fit" and how it relates to your situation. How good is your P−E fit, that is, how much is your job and the organisation still a good match with you and your values now? Are you experiencing any conflict between values? Is your mind/head saying one thing and your heart saying another? Are you able to resolve this conflict?

42

- Do you want to return to your job when you recover? If so, what changes do you need to make in order to remain being true to yourself, as much as possible and is appropriate, when you do return? Do you need to seek clarification regarding your role(s) and responsibilities?
- Identify any areas/situations etc. that you feel you would like to be more assertive in. Do you have someone you can practise your skills safely with, whilst you develop them? Do you know someone, who you can trust, who you consider more assertive, and appropriately assertive (neither submissive nor aggressive) who you could ask to help you, if this is an issue for you?
- I found reading books helpful, as mentioned, but now we also have tutorials on YouTube and so on, for developing assertiveness now.
- Regularly practising mindfulness and/or meditation helps me continue to be true to myself and take action with regard to my values and assertiveness.
- I benefited from professional support. It may be appropriate for you to seek therapy (see Resources) or coaching. If you are interested in coaching, see my website www.thecompassiondoctor.com.

KEY FOUR: BE KIND TO YOURSELF

We can never obtain peace in the outer world
until we make peace with ourselves.
Dalai Lama

What do I mean by "be kind to yourself"?
To understand what it means to be kind, we can first look at some of
the synonyms of the word "kind", such as considerate,
understanding, gentle and compassionate (Collins English
Dictionary, 2020). This gives us an idea of how we need to treat
ourselves in order to demonstrate self-kindness. However, for the
purpose of this key, I am using kindness as an umbrella term for two
specific and closely related concepts, which will be the main focus of
this key, namely self-acceptance and self-compassion. Briefly, to
accept ourselves means that we hold a positive attitude about
ourselves and we recognise not only what might be considered as our
positive qualities, but also our negative ones (Ryff, 1995). The
simplest definition of self-compassion is "compassion directed
inward" (Germer & Neff, 2013).

The concepts of self-acceptance and self-compassion, along with
kindness, are so interconnected that I include them together, even
though they are each rather large topics themselves and have both
been extensively researched. An example of this is that having self-
compassion is perceived as the secret to accepting oneself (Jinpa,
2015). Similarly, it has been said that being compassionate towards
oneself involves, to an extent, having an attitude of acceptance
towards our limitations and faults (Zhang et al., 2019). Equally, being
kind and accepting of oneself is what self-compassion has also been
described as (Holden, Rollins & Gonzalez, 2020). Moreover, "self-
kindness" is one of the three fundamental components of Neff's
(2003) model of self-compassion, which has been extensively
researched. There are a number of other concepts linked to these,
which I will also include briefly, within this key, due to their relevance
in relation to burnout recovery, namely forgiveness and emotional
intelligence (EI).

The importance of self-kindness and cultivating self-acceptance and self-compassion

The majority of the research into kindness has investigated the effects of being kind to others (e.g. Curry et al., 2018) or it has been included as part of research into self-compassion, for example. There is some research though which has shown that there are benefits of self-kindness, such that it can increase our happiness and thus our well-being (e.g. Rowland & Curry, 2018). However, it has also been reported that some people, particularly those who have spent the majority of their lives being critical of themselves, can experience challenges with regard to learning to be kind to themselves, and in such cases practising mindfulness and compassion for oneself can instead be more appropriate (Dreisoerner, Junker & van Dick, 2020).

In contrast, there is a great deal of research to support the benefits of cultivating acceptance and compassion for oneself. I will briefly outline the research here, but more is included further on (see Research Box). Self-acceptance is one of the six concepts vital for general psychological well-being (Ryff, 1989/1995). To accept oneself necessarily includes being willing and able to allow others to see who we truly are, our authentic selves (Carson & Langer, 2006) (the focus of the third key). A lack of self-acceptance can cause us issues, such that it may result in a number of emotional problems, including difficultly controlling our anger, in addition to experiencing depression (Carson & Langer, 2006). Some researchers have also found a link between depression, perfectionism (see below) and reduced levels of self-acceptance (Flett, Besser, Davis & Hewitt, 2003).

Conversely, if we are accepting of ourselves, it enhances our relationships, because as we accept all aspects of ourselves, including our shortcomings, we are more able to accept them in others (Zhang et al., 2019). Self-acceptance has also been found to be an important part of the burnout recovery process (e.g. Salminen et al., 2015), as I personally discovered too. Equally, self-compassion has been found to be connected to our mental well-being (Neff, Knox, Long & Gregory, 2020). In addition, there is evidence to support that being compassionate towards ourselves is linked to our physical well-being too (Hall, Row, Wuensch & Godley, 2013).

We can develop self-compassion, as it is a skill, one that can benefit us by helping us to cope with stress and anxiety in everyday life (Egan, Manzios & Jackson, 2017). Furthermore, it not only increases our ability to cope but it also improves our resilience (Neff et al., 2020). This may be because another benefit is that being compassionate towards ourselves is considered a helpful tool to assist us to cope with our emotions and is thus linked to EI (Neff, 2003) (described in the first key). EI, and effective emotion-management, is therefore an important aspect of managing our well-being. Some researchers, for example, have found that EI helps protect us against burnout and that it can even reduce it (Vlachou, Damigos, Lyrakos et al., 2016). Similarly, there is mounting evidence to support that people with greater compassion for themselves experience less burnout (e.g. Barnard and Curry, 2011).

Hence, when we focus on being kind to ourselves, cultivating self-acceptance and self-compassion, it helps us to be more inclined to support ourselves in other ways, such as implementing the changes needed to restore our body, live our heart-felt values, assert our boundaries and make time for leisure activities and social connection, as described in the other keys, as I have personally found. Others have also reported that learning self-acceptance as part of their burnout recovery helped them be more assertive and have greater respect for themselves (Salminen et al., 2015). In summary, it appears that if we focus on being kind to ourselves, we are perhaps more likely to manage a better ratio between working, resting, playing and socialising, for example.

The value of mindfulness
Mindfulness, referred to in previous keys, is another vast subject and thus I only include a few short paragraphs on it here, focusing on how it relates to this particular key. The origins of mindfulness are based within Buddhism and its meditation practices (Thompson, Arnkoff, & Glass, 2011). Jon Kabat-Zinn is credited with helping mindfulness become established within the West, and particularly with regard to applying it within healthcare settings, due to its benefits including helping people more effectively manage pain, stress and anxiety. He devised the eight-week MBSR programme, which has a great deal of research evidence to support it now (e.g. Janssen et al., 2018), and this is something I have personally benefited from. There is also now a great deal of evidence in support of the benefits of mindfulness not only on health and well-being but also on relationships and other factors (e.g. Wachs & Cordova, 2007).

There are many different definitions of mindfulness. The one I personally find useful describes it as a moment by moment process of being fully aware of what we are experiencing, "observing and attending to the changing field of thoughts, feelings and sensations" (Bishop et al., 2004). As we practise this moment to moment attention, we aim to do it with an attitude that is free from judgement, and instead with openness and acceptance about what we are experiencing in the moment (Thompson et al., 2011). We can also understand more what we mean by mindfulness by contrasting it with what is referred to as "mindlessness", which is what happens when our attention and awareness is all over the place, rather than focused, either ruminating on the past or worrying about the future, which is said to limit our awareness, rather than expand it (Black, 2011).

Furthermore, mindfulness is a fundamental aspect of cultivating self-acceptance because by practising mindfulness, our attention is focused on accepting and exploring present moment experience, instead of evaluating or criticising ourselves (Carson & Langer, 2006). Additionally, mindfulness is important with regard to cultivating compassion for oneself, as it forms one of the three fundamental components of self-compassion (Neff, 2003). Thus, it is a necessary part of helping us to foster compassion for ourselves. Therefore, in order to be kind to ourselves, to cultivate self-acceptance and self-compassion, we can use mindfulness as a tool to help us to do this; again, this is something I have used, and continue to use myself for this purpose.

A note on perfectionism
Perfectionism is another vast topic that has been extensively researched. Although there are some positive aspects of perfectionism, depending on which type it is (which is beyond the scope of this book), it can also cause us problems. It is included here briefly, as it relates to this key and burnout and, as I mentioned in the first key, is an aspect of my personality that I am aware of, which is connected to my workaholic tendencies (the "responsible-workaholic" pattern I referred to previously). Perfectionists have a tendency to strive for perfection, particularly in relation to work. It can also be linked to being critical of oneself, doubting oneself and feeling not good enough (Richardson, Trusty & George, 2018), all negative aspects of perfectionism that I have personally experienced over the years.

There are many examples in the research demonstrating that perfectionists struggle with self-acceptance and that it makes them susceptible to psychological issues at times, including depression (Flett et al., 2003), as previously mentioned. Additionally, a link has been found between perfectionism and burnout, such that perfectionists are at a greater risk of burning out than people who are not (Taris, Van Beek & Schaufeli, 2010). Hence, it has been suggested it is paramount that perfectionists should aim to develop more acceptance of themselves (Flett et al., 2003). In addition, self-compassion is important for people who have particularly high levels of what is described as "self-critical perfectionism" because it has been found that less depression and burnout is experienced by individuals with greater levels of compassion for themselves (Richardson et al., 2018).

My first burnout recovery
As soon as I resigned from my job due to burnout and ill-health, I felt bereft. I had defined myself by my work and work-related achievements for so long. Additionally, I lost my "good-time party girl" identity too. So, one of the main aspects of my recovery consisted of learning to accept myself and where I was. This involved raising my awareness (as described in the first key) of when I was being critical of myself and change that. It included a process of forgiveness too. I had to forgive myself for how I had treated myself, for ignoring my intuition, and later my bodily signals, for not pushing for clarity regarding my roles and responsibilities, for not standing up for myself and asserting my boundaries, and most of all, for trying to be perfect and pushing myself beyond my limits.

Learning to accept myself and be kind and compassionate towards myself was an ongoing process. I found some aspects more challenging than others. I found it challenging to be kind and compassionate towards myself after I had taken a step backwards on my recovery journey, such as getting drunk one night with a friend after I had vowed to abstain from drinking until I had made a full recovery, due to the detrimental effects of alcohol for me mentally and physically, for example. This, and other factors, led me to include the following advice on accepting yourself in my first book:

> It is therefore particularly important to accept yourself and where you are on your journey and treat yourself as you would an innocent child who is just learning to walk. Be kind and gentle with yourself and praise yourself for the steps you are taking. (Buchan, 2008)

My recovery journey also led to me finding out about spirituality, and I read a number of books on the subject and attended a retreat. These are elements which helped make the process of cultivating self-acceptance and self-compassion easier, and practising meditation was a key factor in this process.

One area in my recovery which I thought at the time was appropriate, but in hindsight I have learnt that it actually had a detrimental effect on me, and I now understand why, was in relation to self-esteem. Part of my recovery involved focusing on boosting my self-esteem through therapy and self-development and so on, because I had become consciously aware I had feelings of inadequacy often (though not in all contexts) and at that time, I thought if I boosted my self-esteem, I would finally feel good enough. Nevertheless, it meant that I was still driven to achieve, no matter what (which was in part fuelled by the need and desire to earn money again).

Consequently, even though I had made some progress but did not feel fully recovered and had begun my career retraining in psychology by doing the degree, my dominant mind drove me to take on a part-time course on top of the degree, to train as a massage therapist. I rationalised I could earn money doing that whilst I was still retraining. It also then drove me to undertake a course in NLP, hypnotherapy and coaching, which took place one weekend a month, during the final year of my degree. Then, as soon as that course and the degree ended, I did another (albeit brief) – spirituality-related training! Although these would be considered sensible courses of action for anyone wanting to change careers and set themselves up in private practice offering a variety of therapies, for someone like myself, still recovering from burnout and other health issues, it was detrimental. It meant that I was still being driven to achieve and had issues with perfectionism, which continued over the years, and consequently, partly led to the second burnout.

My second burnout recovery
By the time I experienced the second burnout, my thinking had evolved regarding the subject of self-esteem. Consequently, I have come to agree with the opinion of certain others (e.g. Ellis, 1996; Ryan & Brown, 2003; Thompson & Waltz, 2008) that there are risks involved with self-esteem as it involves evaluating our worth, which can have negative consequences on us, as my experience illustrates. Thus, it is better for our psychological well-being to cultivate self-acceptance instead. Similarly, it is better for our health and well-

being to cultivate self-compassion rather than self-esteem (Neff, 2011). This shift in my thinking about self-esteem, that is, not focusing on it at all, rather focusing on compassion and acceptance instead, has been one of the most significant aspects of my recovery from burnout (and in maintaining my well-being). This is because it has finally enabled me to no longer be driven by the tyranny of my workaholic and critical perfectionistic tendencies, and instead to experience peace with myself.

Therefore, rather than work on my self-esteem as part of my second recovery, I focused on being kind to myself, enhancing my self-acceptance and self-compassion. I found this was essential because I was initially very critical towards myself for burning out again, given I knew about awareness, the importance of taking care of my body, and my soul (i.e. my heart-related core values) and how detrimental it is to ignore all of that and allow my head to dominate my life. I also berated myself for neglecting something that I had considered to be essential to my well-being since the first burnout – my mindfulness/meditation practice.

Furthermore, I became consciously aware that a lack of self-acceptance, and self-compassion, was partly the reason I ignored the part of me that needed a break following the doctorate, and instead, took the job that resulted in me burning out again. I consider that this was partly to do with the fact that being chronically stressed (and thus chronic activation of the SNS) meant that I was stuck in "threat" mode. Thus, I responded from the habitual pattern of "responsible-workaholic", driven to achieve, and driven by fear – fear of missing out what I perceived then as my only opportunity of developing a career in the NHS. I was unable to think of other, more creative solutions. Now that I have an awareness of this element of neuroscience, I can see that it would have been better for me to have not made any decisions about my future at that point. In contrast, it would have been better for me to have taken some time out to activate the PNS by resting, relaxing and practising self-compassion. Nevertheless, I did not have the awareness then and thus the second burnout.

Consequently, I once again worked on forgiving myself for ignoring my body and heart and soul, in favour of my head. Accepting myself this time also included accepting that, as much as I had really wanted to be a part of it, I no longer fitted with the NHS and the system that it had become by then. It included accepting I had (and have) to be true to myself and my heart-felt core values for my inner peace and well-being. It meant accepting that working as a therapist in private practice was no longer for me either. This resulted in me having to let go of my identity as a counselling psychologist and the career that I had worked so hard and for so long to achieve.

I experienced a process of grieving and of letting go. I drew on my spirituality and what I refer to as "feeding my soul". I returned to mindfulness and meditation and I practised self-compassion. I journaled. I had internal dialogues with parts of myself. I also spent a lot of time walking in nature and meditating out in nature. Similarly, I spent time making my heart sing (as I explain in the fifth key) and having let go of the past, I started to explore what I wanted to do, that was connected to my heart-felt values, with the next chapter of my life. Part of that included realising I wanted to return to writing and share what I had learnt through my experiences for the benefit of others, hence writing this book and formalising my training in mindfulness and compassion.

Research Box:

A study investigating the relationship between mindfulness and burnout in teachers suggests that higher levels of self-acceptance (along with mindfulness practice) might not only reduce stress, but also assist in the prevention and/or recovery from burnout (Sun, Wang, Wan & Huang, 2019). In their research into a rehabilitation from burnout programme, one of four main themes reported by participants in their recovery process was "approval". This theme involved the participants learning self-acceptance and self-approval. They reported that this not only helped in regard to their issues with perfectionism, which was linked to their burnout, but it also helped them to become more assertive and take action to make work-related changes (Salminen et al. 2015).

Some of the participants in the study into burnout reported that what made their burnout worse was feeling inadequate, with regard to their professional role (Abedini et al., 2018), which I relate to, particularly in relation to my first burnout experience, as mentioned. In contrast, research into a mindful self-compassion intervention to increase self-compassion in healthcare workers, suggests that it could be a useful method of not only increasing well-being but also in decreasing burnout in this population (Neff et al., 2020).

A pilot study investigating the relationship between self-compassion, self-kindness and other constructs in community nurses found the reduced burnout levels were associated with greater levels of compassion for oneself (Durkin, Beaumont, Martin, & Carson, 2016), for example. Similarly, an investigation into self-compassion, and other concepts, in student midwives found that individuals who reported reduced levels of burnout, and compassion fatigue, reported higher levels of compassion for themselves and greater levels of well-being (Beaumont, Durkin, Hollins Martin & Carson, 2016).

There is also a great deal of research in the psychology literature regarding emotions and the management of them, in relation to well-being, with some relating to burnout and some concerning the importance of self-compassion. An example of such research includes a study into work-related burnout within UK dentistry (Nangle, Henry, von Hippel & Kjelsaas, 2019). The researchers found an association between significantly elevated levels of burnout and emotion dysregulation, that is, the difficulty of managing emotions. This information highlights how important it is to be able to manage difficult emotions well, as mentioned previously.

Additionally, in a study into burnout and emotion regulation in doctors, researchers found there was a correlation between these two and concluded that managing emotions is a significant psychological characteristic linked to burnout (Jackon-Kuku & Grime, 2019). They also found an association between a decrease in burnout and the use of skills to manage emotions, including using mindfulness and other interventions, for example.

Similarly, research into factors promoting recovery from burnout in internal medical residents in the USA, found that being able to process emotionally difficult work-related events, in addition to celebrating their success, with their co-residents through facilitated conversations, was important (Abedini et al., 2018).

There is research to suggest that the more compassionate we are towards ourselves, the better able we are to effectively manage our emotions (Inwood & Ferrari, 2018) for example. Equally, a study into burnout and well-being in anaesthesiologists also reported the importance of emotion regulation strategies, and this included cultivating self-compassion (in addition to mindfulness and other approaches) as research has demonstrated that these approaches reduce burnout and enhance stress management (Lapa et al., 2017). It has also been reported that a benefit of being compassionate towards ourselves is that it enables us to not only more effectively manage our uncomfortable emotions, but it also helps us manage psychological distress and physical pain (Holden et al., 2020).

Tips for being kind to yourself:

Here are some of the strategies that I have found particularly useful with regard to learning to be kind to myself, some of which have already been mentioned:

- Raise your awareness (as per the first key) of how kind you are to yourself currently, by keeping a diary for one week. Reflect on what you recorded. What do you notice in terms of how self-critical and/or judgemental you were compared to how kind or self-accepting?
- Also, become aware of whether you had thought you had issues with self-esteem, not feeling good enough? If so, are you willing to abandon working on that and instead focus on cultivating self-acceptance and self-compassion?
- It can be helpful to practise forgiveness as part of being kind to yourself. What, if anything, do you need to forgive yourself for? What do you need in order to be able to do that? You may want to journal about it.
- Begin to treat yourself as you would a close friend you care about, as part of being kind to yourself. Be gentle with yourself, be understanding, be caring.
- Practise mindfulness. If you would like to learn mindfulness or how to meditate, do contact me at www.thecompassiondoctor.com
- Seek professional psychotherapy or counselling support if you need to (especially if you have a history of trauma in your life) (see Resources).
- Attend a workshop or have one-to-one coaching (see www.thecompassiondoctor.com).
- Remember it is an ongoing process that takes time and it is a continuum rather than an end point to aim for, so be patient with yourself.

54

KEY FIVE: MAKE YOUR HEART SING

Happiness is not something readymade.
It comes from your own actions.
Dalai Lama

What do I mean by "make your heart sing"?
I explained previously in this book that we often talk about "positive" or "negative" emotions, although I personally prefer using the terms "comfortable" or "uncomfortable" instead. However, for the purpose of this key, it is more appropriate to use the former terms that are more commonly used, because making your heart sing involves you proactively cultivating positive emotions. Generally, as adults going about our daily lives, focusing on meeting our many commitments and responsibilities, we listen to our logical, rational minds and act accordingly. We do not consider it important to make time to proactively cultivate positive emotions and we ignore our heart and what it may want or need. Hence, we may find ourselves responding emotionally to whatever is going on in our lives.

Sometimes we can find ourselves experiencing positive emotions, but often, especially if we are experiencing chronic stress or burnout, we find ourselves experiencing negative emotions, which can, in turn, overwhelm us, as I personally experienced. This may be because negative emotions are perceived as more intense and draw our attention more than positive emotions (Fredrickson, Cohn, Coffey, Pek & Finkel, 2008). Furthermore, with regard to burnout, it is perceived to not only emerge from a lack of meaning, as explained in the third key, but it is also closely connected with a lack of joy (Strümpfer, 2003), which is one of the positive emotions I strongly link with making your heart sing.

Why making your heart sing is important
A significant aspect of making your heart sing is cultivating not only joy, as mentioned, but other positive emotions too. There is a main theory in the psychology literature on positive emotions and that is described as the "broaden and build" theory (Fredrickson, 1998). The broaden and build theory subsequently included 10 positive emotions, chosen due to their research support and because people

experience them with relative frequency in everyday life (Fredrickson, 2001). I have focused on the ones that relate to my experience of burnout recovery particularly, and/or what has been reported in the research, namely joy (or happiness), inspiration, gratitude and serenity.

Please also note that whilst love is included in Fredrickson's 10 emotions, I reference it only briefly in this key. This is because, even though love (that is learning to love myself, find activities that I loved, and at some point, falling in love) formed a significant part of my first recovery, I wrote extensively about this in my first book (see Buchan, 2008). Additionally, whilst love from others formed part of my second recovery too, my thinking evolved in between burnouts and what was more important in the second recovery was re-connecting with my values (as described in the third key) and self-acceptance and self-compassion (see the fourth key). Furthermore, there is more evidence to support these later concepts (at least compared to self-love) in the psychology literature, regarding burnout recovery and well-being.

It is important to make your heart sing by cultivating positive emotions because of the many benefits associated with them. Positive emotions help us to expand or broaden our thoughts and our behaviours, and as a result, we increase or build mental, physical and social resources (Fredrickson, 1998). Joy, for example, according to the "broaden and build" theory, helps us to expand as it creates the inclination "to play, push the limits and be creative" (Strümpfer, 2003). Another benefit of positive emotions, it is said, is that they reverse persistent negative emotions, in addition to fuelling and building resilience (Fredrickson, 2001).

Moreover, in an article on burnout and resilience, positive emotions have been described as one of five psychological concepts that can be helpful, not only in preventing burnout, but equally in assisting people in burnout recovery (Strümpfer, 2003). Similarly, in a study into work-related burnout and positive emotions, researchers found the more that positive emotions were experienced, the less burnout was experienced (Gong, Schooler, Wang & Tao, 2018). In short, positive emotions have been found to not only enhance our psychological well-being, but also our physical well-being too (Gong et al., 2018). Further research on positive emotions is included in the Research Box. Thus, whilst negative emotions do have their uses, and we need to manage them effectively, we also need to be proactive in cultivating positive emotions because they are important with regard to recovery from burnout, but also for general well-being and to flourish in life.

A note on passion

It is natural, given its association with the heart, that we think of passion when we consider making our hearts sing. Passion means different things to different people, and the meaning changes depending on the context. With regard to work, we are urged to find our passion, and do what we love, with the belief, or promise, that then we will never "work" another day in our lives again – the implication being that because we enjoy doing it so much, it will not feel like work. However, there are potential dangers with this, especially if we are recovering from burnout. It has been said, for example, that even people whose work is their passion can experience burnout, and their lives can become out of balance (Donahue et al., 2012).

This is particularly the case regarding "obsessive passion", which is when we are compelled to do the activity we are passionate about, so rather than it feeling like a choice; we feel we cannot live without engaging in it, and thus it causes a negative effect in our lives. In contrast "harmonious passion" is not compulsive, so we choose to do the passionate activity freely, and although it is important to us, it does not overpower us or dominate our lives, and thus it does not have the same negative consequences (Vallerand et al., 2003). I include this here as it is something I personally have to be mindful of, given my workaholic (and other) tendencies that I have previously described. Hence, when I was initially recovering from burnout (both times), I focused on doing activities that sparked enjoyment and other positive emotions, purely for their own sake and my well-being, rather than trying to find a "passion" in life, to subsequently make a new career out of. Therefore, the remainder of the key focuses on two main aspects of making your heart sing, by cultivating positive emotions, namely making time for leisure activities, and social connection.

Make time for leisure activities

There are a number of positive emotions that are included in Fredrickson's (2001) "broaden and build" theory, which were particularly relevant regarding my burnout experiences, which I will focus on in connection with leisure activities. Although I refer to them separately here, this is for simplicity only, because in reality they can overlap, such that when I feel inspired, for example, it also makes me feel joyful.

Joy

Prior to my first burnout, when I was experiencing chronic stress, I spent the majority of my time and energy on my work, whether that was in work itself, or in my non-work time, such as doing the A-level course in Portuguese to try and learn the language. Although some people may find that doing such a course would bring them joy, it was not the case for me. This is because, as I explain in my story, it did not spark heart-felt joy in the same way as anything Spanish-related, for numerous reasons. Additionally, because I was spending so much time "in my head" when at work, I now realise I needed to spend my off-work time doing something totally unrelated to that, and something that helped me to mentally switch off (see Research Box for more on this).

The same could also be said for my second burnout. The boundaries for that role were more blurred because, along with delivering therapy and other NHS-related tasks, it included a training element, which meant attending lectures and studying at home. Consequently, when I was not spending time on those activities, which consumed most of my time and energy, I was so exhausted I mostly just tried to rest. Although I did experience joy and laughter in relation to the second experience, which was largely due to the great people I met in the role, it was not enough to reverse the effects of all the negative emotions I was feeling the rest of the time, due to the challenges. Thus, both recoveries included regaining joy in my life.

Another word for joy is happiness, as mentioned. So, to cultivate this and make our hearts sing, we need to find what makes us feel joyful and happy, because as with so many things, it is very subjective. Sometimes we have moments that are unplanned that we find trigger joy in us. But, when these are lacking, we can help ourselves and our recovery by doing activities that bring us joy. The things that I associate with joy and happiness are play and laughter. We can find these in the small things in life, as well as larger ones. As with most of these aspects, it is a question of experimenting, especially if we have neglected this aspect of our lives due to prioritising work and so on. Once we have identified what brings us joy, and ideally that would be a number of activities so that we have options, we need to ensure we make time to include one or more of those in our lives regularly.

Inspiration

Inspiration is another of the positive emotions included in the "broaden and build" theory (Fredrickson, 2001) which I lacked in relation to both burnout experiences. Again, both my roles were lacking in inspiration and due to prioritising work above everything else, I did not make time to find inspiration in my non-work time. It was by accident, rather than design, that I discovered how important inspiration was to my well-being and what inspired me in regard to the first experience. The second time, I was very consciously aware of what inspired me, and it was neglecting activities that make me feel inspired that was also a part of the burnout, and so I ensured my recovery included that. The great benefit of taking the time to connect with what makes us feel inspired, and thus cultivate it, is that it can really help us to feel uplifted during challenging times, such as dealing with burnout. As with joy, if we have forgotten, or are unaware of, what makes us feel inspired, we need to experiment.

Serenity

Following on from the above, serenity is another of the positive emotions included in the "broaden and build" theory (Fredrickson, 2001) which I lacked in relation to both burnout experiences. I lacked moments of feeling peaceful and calm in relation to the first experience in particular. It was a rather alien concept to me, having only experienced very brief moments of it during a short course of yoga. Even after I discovered meditation and enjoyed the peace and quiet on a retreat during my first recovery, a part of me was still put off by this emotion. I thought that if I cultivated more moments of serenity in my life, I would miss the excitement and adrenaline rush that accompanies the drama of life. This made practising mindfulness very challenging during my first eight-week MBSR course!

However, by the time I reached the second burnout, I had a much greater understanding of the benefits of serenity and had experienced how good feeling peaceful and serene feels many times. Hence, I naturally included this as part of my second recovery journey, through the practice of mindfulness and meditation, but also via spending time in what is referred to as "restorative places" (Strümpfer, 2003). My restorative places include a favourite spot by the coast, certain areas of forest or woodland, in addition to large parks where there is minimal traffic. I also find being in a church or in the meditation room of a Buddhist centre or monastery, when there is no service going on, very restorative and serenity inducing.

The sense of connection with something larger than myself that I feel when I am in these restorative places makes my heart sing. Equally though, I can experience this at home, first thing in the morning before most people are awake, which is useful especially if we are unable to travel or do not have access to these sorts of places for whatever reason. Furthermore, I make use of the power of visualisation and the ability we have to mentally transport ourselves in our mind to places that we have visited before that we feel restores us.

There is neuroscientific research for example, which shows that using our imagination in certain ways may influence us mentally and physically in a manner that is important with regard to well-being (Reddan, Wager & Schiller, 2018). Therefore, I have not only used my imagination through visualisation in relation to restorative places, but I have also used it for other aspects of my burnout recovery journey, due to the benefits of this.

Once more, it is a case of experimenting if we do not know what makes us feel peaceful, whilst also noticing if any part of us is reluctant or fearful of cultivating serenity in our lives, and including these activities in our lives in some way.

Gratitude
Gratitude is the final one of the positive emotions from Fredrickson's (2001) "broaden and build" theory that I am including in this key. In my family, as was common at that time, we were brought up to "be grateful" but it was more of an injunction, something we "should" think, and something we "should" demonstrate through action, rather than as something that was a positive emotion that would make our hearts sing. Thus, as with inspiration, I discovered by accident the importance of gratitude in relation to well-being, as a result of watching Oprah on TV during my first recovery, as I explain later. Nevertheless, many years have passed since then and now there is a wealth of research to support the benefits of gratitude (see Research Box). Moreover, there is a simple activity that we can do to cultivate gratitude, which is also evidence-based, namely identifying and recording "three good things" each day (Lai & O'Carroll, 2017). Consequently, this is an easy activity to start with. My second recovery expanded on this.

Make time for social connection

We are social beings, as mentioned previously, and connecting with others is important to our psychological and physical well-being. Social connection is, for example, one of the six factors essential for general psychological well-being, which is described as having positive relationships with others (Ryff, 1995). This is because we have a psychological need to belong, which motivates us to develop and sustain enduring positive and important relationships with others (Baumeister & Leary, 1995). We fulfil this need by making time for social connection. In general, developing and maintaining relationships with others has the benefit of producing positive emotions, whereas an absence of interpersonal relationships is associated with an increase in mental and physical issues (Baumeister & Leary, 1995).

However, issues experienced in regard to interpersonal relationships can also have a negative impact on our well-being, as I personally experienced in connection with my first burnout. Moreover, my workaholic tendencies also negatively impacted the relationship with my husband. This is because it meant I prioritised work over not only nurturing myself, but also above nurturing our relationship. This is unsurprising given that research into workaholism and relationships has found workaholics neglected their intimate relationship and that this resulted in a decrease in the quality and satisfaction of their relationship (Bakker, Demerouti & Burke, 2009).

Returning to positive relationships with others, which is the focus here in regard to making our heart sing, it has also been suggested that these "quality ties" in particular, can help us with preventing burnout, and also to survive, or recover from it (Strümpfer, 2003). This is particularly the case regarding relationships with those we love. This is because love is fundamental for our survival as human beings and it helps us to manage situations that cause us stress, and thus it is considered a vital part of a life that is good and healthy (Esch & Stefano, 2005). Hence, it is really important to make time for social connection, as part of making our hearts sing, to support our burnout recovery and have more of a balance in life in relation to work and non-work time.

The difference between the focus of the previous section in this key, and this section on social connection is that the former focuses on us as individuals, whilst the focus here is on us in relation to other people, although the aim of both is to cultivate positive emotions.

Therefore, the emphasis is on doing social activities, activities that involve others which make our heart sing. Ideally these activities are done face-to-face, but when this is not possible, virtual social connection is better than no social connection. What we choose to do concerning social connection depends on a variety of things, including whether or not we are in a relationship and just need to invest some time in nurturing that, or if we are single and requiring to fulfil the need to belong, so connecting with people who are like-minded, and have similar values is important, for example. Again, it is a question of raising our awareness (as described in the first key), considering our situation and circumstances, and identifying what we feel we need and committing to make time for that.

My first burnout recovery

To recover from my first burnout, after I had worked on restoring my body so that I had more energy, and done some mental and emotional processing, I then sought to make my heart sing by focusing on having fun! I had always loved musical theatre and singing (just for the pure joy of it) and I was lucky to find an evening class locally. What was great about the musical theatre course was that I was learning but there was no exam at the end and most people were there just to have fun. It was the first time in years I had allowed myself to do such an activity, that is, one just for the fun of it. There was minimal actual connection with others due to me arriving and leaving promptly as I was still having to be mindful of my energy levels. But, it was great for fostering joy and inspiration, in addition to love, as I loved the activity. I looked forward to practising at home when I had the house to myself too.

I also discovered the benefit of gratitude, and began to keep a gratitude journal, which assisted me in the process of changing my mindset and it made my heart sing. I sought to cultivate serenity and taught myself meditation too, as part of my recovery, as explained previously. Similarly, this was linked to my discovering spirituality as part of my recovery journey, through watching Oprah and discovering the field of "mind, body and spirit", which I also found very inspiring and gave me hope that I could recover.

Having experienced such a shift in my life as a result of burnout, leaving work, having therapy, discovering spirituality and so on, I was keen to meet people who were like-minded. I was, I realise in hindsight, looking for the sense of belonging that I felt was missing as a result of leaving my career and my old identity. This led me to attend talks at Alternatives in London (as mentioned previously). There would be a different speaker each week from the field of "mind, body, spirit". I found the talks very uplifting and I met people who were interested in the same topics as I was (psychology, self-help, spirituality, health and well-being etc.) who were attending, but also I met the people who volunteered there, who helped run the events. I subsequently became a member of their volunteer team, because not only did it provide me with a sense of meaning in my life as I was contributing, but it also gave me the social connection I needed.

Then, whilst doing my undergraduate degree in psychology and counselling, I met (via the internet) a psychology student attending another university who was also trying to recover from chronic fatigue (though not in relation to work-related burnout). We ended up dating for about 18 months. During that time, I experienced a great deal of positive emotion, particularly love, happiness and inspiration, as we were both committed to learning all that we could about how to recover and enhance well-being. Moreover, the relationship gave me a great sense of belonging as we cared for each other equally and we understood what each other was going through, and our visions for the future. In addition, I spent time with the few close friends who stood by me in spite of my health issues and the changes in my life. Consequently, I personally experienced the benefits of social connection (once I had the energy) in relation to my first burnout recovery.

My second burnout recovery
I prioritised restoring my body to recover from burnout the second time too, as I explained in the second key. Equally, I was aware I felt my soul had been eroded to an extent, as described in the third key, and so my other priority was what I would describe as "repairing my soul" and returning to myself. I spent time doing the leisure activities that generated feelings of joy and inspiration, such as spending time in nature, reading books and watching comedies. I also returned to writing, which is an activity I love but had neglected, and this included doing a creative writing course for fun, not as part of an academic or career pathway. Once we re-located to the south coast, I then focused on serenity too, returning to meditation and a regular mindfulness practice.

This time I was (and still am) happily married. We had both been aware for a while, prior to me burning out, that we were not spending the time together that we both really wanted, due to me prioritising work, and so we re-addressed this as soon as I had taken some time to recharge myself and we'd settled in our new home. My husband's unconditional love and support were of great help to me too, particularly with his patience and understanding about burning out again, and the fact that I had not heeded his warning about taking on the NHS job. Similarly, I had spent little time with family and my close friends and so I made time to catch up with them too. Furthermore, once we relocated, I found a sense of belonging with the local dog-walking community, thanks to our dog Tommy. Thus, like others who have overcome burnout (see Research Box), my second recovery included cultivating positive emotions through leisure activities and making time for social connection in my life again.

Research Box:

Positive emotions

Neuroscience has found support for the benefits of positive emotions in general, such that they are perceived as contributing to our emotional and physical health, with meditation, flow activities and activities involving contemplation being ways found to foster positive emotions (Alexander et al., 2021). Additionally, positive emotions were induced via a loving kindness meditation by participants in one study, which found that this increased the frequency they experienced them over time, which led to increases in support from others and purpose in life, in addition to a reduction in symptoms relating to health issues (Fredrickson, Cohn, Coffey, Pek & Finkel, 2008).

With regard to gratitude, in a review by Wood, Froh & Geraghty (2010), they found people can experience gratitude as a result of receiving assistance from other people and by regularly practising appreciation for the good things in life, and that both of these are strongly connected to well-being. There is research to support that gratitude can be cultivated by the activity of regularly recording things we are grateful for and that this can enhance our well-being (Lai & O'Carroll, 2017). Others have also found that counting our blessings or thinking about what we are grateful for in our lives can increase gratitude and thus well-being (Chan, 2010).

In addition to the wealth of research supporting the association between positive emotions and well-being in general, there is some research linking positive emotions, and activities that generate them, and recovery from burnout. In the study by Abedini et al. (2018) for example, they found that although taking time off from work was important for recovery (which is a part of rebalancing), other activities were also helpful so that they felt there was more to their life than their work, including leisure activities, such as travelling.

Similarly, in another investigation into a rehabilitation programme for burnout, researchers found that at the end of it, individuals reported experiencing having feelings of joy back in their lives again. This also included a renewed interest in hobbies for some of the people (Salminen et al., 2015). In a small, longitudinal qualitative study into job burnout recovery and non-recovery experiences, one of Andreou's (2015) participants reported having "regained joy and spirit" and that the support of others (healthcare workers, family etc.) was a significant aspect of this.

Furthermore, Siu, Cooper and Phillips (2014) presented two interventions aimed at enhancing work-related well-being and reducing burnout in healthcare workers and teachers in Hong Kong in their study, which took a positive psychology approach. The interventions, described as training, encompassed many things, including using positive psychology in the workplace, which included gratitude, in addition to the role of optimism and hope, to enhance stress coping, for example. They found that following the interventions participants reported enhanced well-being and reduced burnout.

Fjellman-Wiklund et al. (2010) researched the experience of patients with burnout at the end of a one-year rehabilitation programme, which included CBT and qi gong for one group, and qi gong only for the other group. Consequently, participants reported having "joy for life" in addition to "faith and hope" in regard to their futures. Finally, in their investigation into burnout experienced by a number of Swedish men and women, Arman et al. (2011) found that some reported part of the burnout recovery included having an increasing gratitude for what they have. Moreover, for some it also encompassed doing a creative activity of their choosing, including reading or spending time in nature.

Leisure activities and social connection
With regard to leisure activities and social connection, researchers have found that people who reported participating in creative leisure activities, including hobbies, along with social activities, also reported many health-related benefits (Winwood, Bakker & Winefield, 2007). Similarly, participating in social activities and other leisure activities, not only low-effort ones but also more active leisure pursuits, has been found to be beneficial for well-being, including enhancing recovery, in this case daily work-recovery (Sonnentag, 2001).

Benefits of the above in relation to burnout have also been reported. Participants in the study into burnout recovery by Abedini et al. (2018) were all able to continue in their jobs whilst experiencing burnout and trying to recover. Some of them reported that their recovery from burnout did include taking some time off and spending time with family and friends, for example. Equally, some of the participants in the research into a burnout rehabilitation programme made changes which included reviving their social connections as part of their recovery (Salminen et al., 2015).

Others have also found that, for people who are experiencing high levels of burnout but are still continuing in their job, pursuing social activity in off-work time is of benefit, due to the chance to have meaningful conversations with people (Oerlemans & Bakker, 2014). Likewise, the benefit of social activity for people experiencing high levels of burnout, and still working, is also that it helps them to switch off from work and aids relaxation (ten Brummelhuis & Bakker, 2012)

Finally, in another investigation into burnout recovery referred to previously, participants in the programme, which included CBT with qi gong, reported that their recovery included reducing their work and spending increased time, not only on themselves, but also with friends and family, which facilitated the building of positive interpersonal relationships (Fjellman-Wiklund et al., 2010).

Tips for making your heart sing:

Here are some tips I have found helpful regarding making your heart sing:

- Schedule in your leisure time. If you are still attending work, schedule some time off if you can. If not, at least allocate some of your non-work time to this. Prioritise some leisure time for yourself above doing chores for example. Seek support from family/friends if you need help to look after children and so on. Then, identify what is it that you want to do for fun, entertainment, inspiration and see if you can begin to start doing one of the activities on your list.
- If you are not sure what activity to do, think back to what you used to enjoy doing as a child, before you became an adult with all the responsibilities that brings – what did you like to do? How easy is it to start doing that again? What would you need to do to make that happen? If money is an issue, is there a way you can still do the activity but at a reduced cost or for free?
- Do some meditation, mindfulness, yoga or other practice that would help you to ground yourself back in your body, and relax you, if you are still finding it challenging to know what makes your heart sing – as it is helpful to loosen the grip of the rational/logical mind for a moment and allow you to access the creative aspect of the brain to find this out. This will also help you cultivate serenity.

- Still not sure? Just experiment. Pick something that you feel drawn to doing – paint, sing, dance, read material that uplifts you, visit your restorative place (physically, virtually or in your mind) – use your imagination. Notice how you feel. Be mindful of any self-criticism or judgements (see the fourth key for help). Do not make this more work for yourself. Have fun with it. If it feels like work, then it may help to work on restoring your body first, until you have more energy for this (see the second key).
- Watch TV and/or films that make you laugh, inspire you or uplift you.
- Keep a gratitude journal. At some point in the day, record a number of things that you genuinely feel grateful for, or deeply appreciate, no matter how small they may seem. Ideally, find something new each day if you can.
- Take some time to connect with family and friends that you have a positive relationship with, and especially those you feel are supportive and uplifting to be around (as soon as you feel ready to – I needed some quality alone time initially during my burnout recovery).

PART TWO: MY PERSONAL STORY

The Historical Background to My Burnout Experiences

Childhood

I come from what is referred to as a predominantly working-class background and most of my family started work at a relatively young age. It was a very different time then. My paternal great grandfather worked away a great deal and so, being the eldest child, my grandfather had to look after the family. He left school and started work aged 14. His family needed the money. During the Second World War, unable to join the forces due to a work-related injury, he did a variety of manual jobs. After the war, on top of his full-time day job as a panel beater, he had an additional job, sometimes working until 10pm and some weekends, until he retired.

My paternal grandmother also worked from a young age and she juggled several jobs at the same time. My father remembers his mother starting her first job as a cleaner at a London university at 6am each day. When she finished there, she would go on to her second job, working in a college canteen, and this was then followed by another cleaning job. My father (an only child) remembers coming home to an empty house, and having to "get the tea on", as both his parents would be out working.

My maternal grandfather started working whilst he was still at school, helping out on a local farm during the school holidays. In his early teens, he worked in a Private Members Club in London, initially as what was referred to then as a "page boy" (a young attendant), then a steward, and finally a dining-room waiter. The hours were long. He would work from 7am to midnight. Later, he worked in a printing shop and learned the trade. He was 24 when the Second World War broke out and he subsequently joined the RAF. During the war, he was captured and spent time in a prisoner of war camp. After the war, he went into partnership and set up a printing company, with a stationery shop. He was never home before 7pm and always worked Saturday mornings and some Sunday mornings, if there was an urgent job. His work was his life, until he retired.

My maternal grandmother was in her teens when she began working in London. After she got married and had my mother (and subsequently my uncle), she worked from home doing upholstery for a well-known retail company, whilst her children were at school.

69

My uncle was only 11 years old when he began working as what was referred to then as a "milk boy", helping a local milkman with his deliveries on Saturdays. At the same time, he used to assist my grandfather at his printing shop in his spare time too, but preferred being outside. He subsequently left school at 15 to work full time as a milkman. He worked six, often seven days a week, for many years, until he retired.

With regard to my mother, she had several Saturday jobs in retail whilst she was at school. Then, at 16, she began full-time work, first in an office, then later in a travel agency. She continued working until she was 24, when she became pregnant with me. Once I started school, she did some occasional part-time work on and off, for a few hours a week. At 38, she had my brother, and some years later, once he started junior school, she had the opportunity to work part-time at his school. And so, for all of my childhood, until my early teens, my father was the principal income earner in our family. Being a very traditional man, that was the way my father preferred it.

Like my uncle, my father was also 11 years old when he began working. He would go to work with his father, outside of school hours, so that my grandfather could teach him his trade as a car panel beater. He subsequently left school at 14 and began working full-time. He was self-employed for many years. The work was very unpredictable, particularly in the 1970s. When he had work, he would make the most of it and work long hours, sometimes until 10pm during the week, and he would also work on Saturday mornings. Then, suddenly, the work would just dry up for a period of time. These were the most stressful times for the whole family. My father found it very difficult and frustrating not having work. It caused my parents a great deal of stress and anxiety.

So, when my father had work, and thus an income, I did not see him much, but he was happier and family life was easier. When he had no work, I saw much more of him, but we experienced financial hardship, with that and the uncertainty of when he would have work again, making him unhappy. Consequently, it made my mother and me unhappy, and family life was extremely stressful and uncomfortable. Given my family's history regarding work and the financial challenges in my childhood (and the impact it had on me, consciously or unconsciously), it is not surprising that I began doing tasks for money from a young age, starting with chores around the house for pocket money (when my parents could afford to give it to me).

When I was 11, my brother was born, and I began my first informal job as a babysitter. For the most part, it was an easy job. However, I also felt a significant sense of responsibility for my brother and at the time, there were reports on the news of infant cot deaths. This made me worry he might die in his sleep, which meant I would constantly check on him throughout the evening, to make sure he was still breathing.

Word of my babysitting services grew amongst my mum's circle of friends and I was soon in demand. I enjoyed earning a bit of money on top of money for chores. I found babysitting easier, the older the children in my care were. But I also found it lonely, as the children were usually in bed by the time I arrived. There were no mobile phones then, so it was just me, and the TV, and still the sense of responsibility I felt for the children in my care.

Early teenage years – school and work
Like others in my family, I also began working part-time when I was still at school, getting my first part-time job at 13 years old, when my parents gave their permission for me to work in the local newsagent's and greengrocers at weekends. It was harder work than babysitting, but I preferred it as I was not responsible for the well-being of "small humans", only products and providing a good service. I loved working with people, giving customers the items they asked for and seeing them happy. My customers expressed gratitude for my help and my boss validated me for doing a good job, for being responsible and reliable. That felt great, as, like most teenagers, that was not my experience at home. Also, like many teens, I enjoyed being out of the house, away from my parents!

The other positives were that it was fun and enjoyable. I learnt a great deal, interacting with people of all ages, thus it was good for my social skills development. As I was then earning my own money, I began to buy my own clothes, with the exception of my school uniform. This meant I learnt how to manage money and respect it, as I had earned it. I learnt to value it (whether rightly or wrongly). Working and earning money gave me a sense of freedom from a young age, particularly the ability to save it and also to spend it on what I wanted. Additionally, my family, and my father in particular, valued work more than education, which is understandable given their history, coming from working-class backgrounds.

At that time, I saw nothing wrong with working at the weekend, in addition to attending school, and even doing the odd babysitting too. As I mentioned, I come from a family of hard workers, so it seemed normal. However, it meant I was doing rather a lot. Moreover, in our family (as is common in Western culture) it was only really acceptable to rest if you were ill, or if you were away on holiday. Although we did not realise it particularly at the time, this busyness and discouragement from rest, along with other factors, began to take its toll on my health. I had frequent sore throats and then, when I was 14, right before my mock exams, I was diagnosed with glandular fever and was off school for weeks.

Before I left school, I returned to part-time work, managing to get my then dream job working for a well-known retail company. It was the "glory days" of the company, when staff were highly valued and treated accordingly, with lots of staff facilities within the store and other perks, which I believe have long since been scrapped, sadly. I juggled this with homework and an increasing social life.

The First Burnout Cycle

Life in balance and a high level of resilience

Although I enjoyed working in retail, I knew I did not want to do it for a career. The problem was, I had no idea what I wanted to do. Also, as a female living where I lived in a relatively low-income area at that time, I was not expected to achieve very much anyway. This combined with a lack of confidence in my abilities (which had, incidentally, been noted by my teacher in my school report when I was about seven!), and my self-doubt regarding passing exams such as A-levels, compounded my lack of career clarity. Thankfully, a chance discussion with a woman I met during my work experience at nearby Heathrow Airport, helped me to discover there were other options for me. She told me I could do an Ordinary National Diploma (OND) in Business and Finance for two years, with course work only, no exams. I could also still work part-time in the retail store. And so that was my next step.

I was enjoying my time on the OND so much, particularly the Tourism and Spanish options, that I wanted to continue on to do the two-year Higher National Diploma (HND) after it. However, at the same time I had become desperate to leave home and experience freedom and greater independence. Consequently, I applied to what was then a Polytechnic in Essex, where I would be able to live in halls of residence. But my path was not straightforward.

At that time, there were no student loans. The government provided grants to some students, but this was not enough to fund the course and the living costs for the two years. We were expected to meet any shortfall. Determined to achieve my goal no matter what, I explored strategies to make it happen. So, after the OND, I took one year out to save up the funding shortfall. I got a full-time job as a marketing assistant in a company that made lifts and I continued working in my retail job in the evenings and on Saturdays (there was no Sunday trading back then for that type of shop).

Juggling a full-time job plus a part-time job on top can be stressful. But, I did not experience it as stressful. I was young and these were low-level positions without much responsibility. I also enjoyed the work I was doing and the places I worked in. I enjoyed the camaraderie, being part of a team. We had good managers and I never felt overworked in either place. We always had an actual hour for lunch in both places and regular breaks. There was a good balance between work and socialising too. The retail staff and I would frequently socialise together after work in the local pub, whereas with the lift company staff, we would often go to the pub at lunchtime together! As I say, they were very different, fun, times. A part of me was sad to resign from my jobs when it was time for me to move to Essex and start the HND, as I had enjoyed working, socialising and earning money.

Having earned my own money and saved, I had an advantage over my peers when I made the move and started the course. I had the power and freedom to choose exactly how to spend my money, unlike my peers who had to ask permission from their parents for extras like field trips to France and Spain. I liked that empowered feeling having my own money gave me. It also meant that for the first time in a long while, I did not have to juggle studying with work.

The two years passed swiftly, and, towards the end of the course, I knew I wanted a career in the travel and tourism industry. I loved languages and travelling abroad felt exciting. However, after graduating, it took a while for me to get a job in the industry. This is because my priorities had shifted. I had fallen in love with a fellow student and we had been dating a while. He planned to return to the Canary Islands, where he was from, after the course. I felt deeply upset when he did not ask me to go with him. Nevertheless, determined to achieve my goal, which in this instance was to continue in the relationship no matter what – I prioritised doing whatever it took to be able to continue to support myself financially, but still be near my boyfriend. I knew if I did an intensive course on how to Teach English as a Foreign Language (TEFL) I would be in with a chance to follow him out there – and so I did.

Some episodes of acute stress but still a good level of resilience

I managed to secure a job in the Canary Islands at an academy teaching English as a foreign language before I moved out. I worked there for a total of two years. When I was not teaching at the English Academy, I taught English privately to supplement my income. I made time to go to the beach and socialise with friends too. I loved many things about teaching, particularly the variety of clients I got to work with, from primary school children to hospital doctors and lawyers. But, a part of me yearned to use my other qualifications and work in travel and tourism. The teaching hours were not very convenient for me either, being mostly early mornings and/or evenings. I also wanted a job I could switch off from when I was not working, rather than having to spend my free time lesson planning and marking homework. Thankfully, a change in location opened up an opportunity.

My boyfriend had since moved to another of the islands in the Canaries, where his family were based. I followed not long after. To cut a long story short, a position became available working as a marketing assistant for a local tourism organisation. I applied, and after a rigorous selection process, all in Spanish, I was overjoyed to hear I'd got the job. It was great to be able to finally put my HND to good use, and my Spanish. It was such a challenging and varied role. I had to deal with the UK travel press, organising press trips and so on, which was initially incredibly challenging, especially when we had any potentially damaging PR incidents, and other tasks. However, I had a good, supportive manager, and I was part of a wider, collaborative team and felt the workload was appropriate. We worked from 8am to 3pm, rarely staying any longer. I even managed to teach English privately some evenings afterwards, to supplement my income, as my tourism job was not well paid.

Whilst my work life was going really well, my personal life was not and several months after getting my dream tourism job, I finally ended my relationship. Around the same time, my manager sent me to the UK to do some promotional work. Being in the UK, and no longer in a relationship, I realised I wanted to move back. So, when a new company was awarded the contract to represent the island in the UK, and they needed a marketing/account assistant, I applied, got the job, and moved back to the UK permanently.

Initially, it was challenging having to adjust to the change in my relationship with my previous boss, and my old colleagues, as they were now "the client". Additionally, although the job was still fun, I had to adjust to the British work culture again. It came as quite a shock after three years of working in the Canary Islands! I found the work was much more demanding, and stressful, especially in the period prior to big events such as the annual travel trade event, and press trips to the island and so on. It meant working in the evenings and at weekends sometimes (for no extra pay). I was so busy that it left me little time to think about my relationship break up. I did not consider myself a "workaholic". I was still relatively young, having fun, and so committed to my work that I was giving it everything.

Plus, it was a small company and that was the culture. It was good to be seen as one of the first people in the office in the mornings, and one of the last to leave each night.

We were like a family too, which helped. We trusted each other and worked really well together. We socialised often together too, whether it was going to the pub for lunch or clubbing after work on Fridays. We frequently "burnt the candle at both ends" too, with work events in the evening, which we would run, then afterwards, we would go out together, drinking and clubbing until the early hours. This would be followed by a few hours' sleep, if you were lucky, and then back in the office on time the following day!

In the time that I was there, I worked my way up to Marketing and PR Manager and really looked forward to going into work each day. But then the owner decided to retire and sell up. Sadly, things were never the same again. One of the sales managers was promoted to director, and the existing director remained in his role – and so for a while, we had two directors. Some people felt loyal to the existing director, others to the newly promoted one and so we ended up with two divided teams on opposite sides – a bit like Brexit! Consequently, office politics became a significant issue. We lost trust in each other. We stopped communicating with each other unless it was absolutely necessary. The work environment became very uncomfortable and quite toxic at times.

I subsequently found myself questioning the point of my job for the first time. I found myself thinking that what I did, did not help people in any deep and meaningful way. I was also experiencing issues in my personal life again, which was causing me stress. I thought that if I had a better understanding of people, then maybe that would help me to cope with both my personal life and my work life. This led me to do a short-term evening course in counselling and psychology. I did not share my extra-curricular activity with my colleagues though. I did not want them to ask me how I was finding it, or to ask me if I had passed my essays. I still lacked confidence in my academic abilities and did not want them to make fun of me.

Additionally, around this time, I experienced another stressor. One night, I got back to the flat I was living in with friends. As I opened the door, I saw that drawers had been emptied and our belongings were scattered all over the place. We had been burgled. It was such a massive shock. I felt violated. I called the police. They told me to check the burglar was not still in the flat! Thankfully, they had gone. I called a close male friend who immediately drove over to be with me, and I proceeded to get drunk, to numb out the shock. This, in addition to the work issues, meant my stress levels were increasing.

Someone suggested I do yoga to help reduce my stress levels. So, I did a six-week course of it at our local yoga centre, which also included some brief meditation. Although I found it relaxing, I was not motivated at that time to continue with either the yoga or the meditation. It had felt more like a welcome short holiday abroad – it was nice for a brief period, but I didn't necessarily want to "live there"!

The toxic work environment continued too. Consequently, when I heard that the organisers of several of the travel trade events were looking for someone to manage the travel and other arrangements of the speakers attending these events on a short-term contract, I jumped at the chance and resigned from my tourism marketing role. I liked being part of a collaborative team again and the job was varied and interesting. But, the closer we got to the actual dates of the events we were organising, the workload and the pressures increased dramatically. It meant working long days and nights and having no life outside of work for several weeks prior to the events.

During the convention and conferences, we were on duty almost 24-7. The work was relentless. I remember at one of the events, myself and one of the technical crew were in the hotel room of one of our VIP speakers until 3am, helping him sort out his speech that he was due to deliver in a few hours' time! There were not only daytime events we were responsible for organising but also events each evening too, which meant hardly any sleep that week. After the closing ceremony, I sat down on the floor in the crew area and just wept! I had suddenly come down off of the "adrenaline-high" I had been experiencing in the run up to, and during, the event, with a massive bump! Thankfully, it did not last and after a proper two-week holiday in a destination unrelated to work, after which I felt fully re-charged and energised, I re-focused my attention on the final, smaller event. In no time at all, my fixed six-month contract had come to an end and I was looking for the next role.

Once more, it seemed luck was on my side as another UK marketing company had secured the contract to represent the island in the Canaries I had previously worked for and they needed someone to manage the account. I spoke to them and, as I was immediately available, we agreed I would do the job until they found someone else for the role, as I did not want to do it long term. Shortly after starting there, due to a member of staff leaving, I found myself managing the account for a major city in Brazil! Again, I found it exciting and challenging at first. I felt so lucky to visit the city twice in such a short space of time, as part of my job.

From acute stress to chronic stress and decreasing levels of resilience

I liked and got on well with my colleagues. However, I did not agree with the management style of our Managing Director/company owner. She was incredibly volatile too. You never knew what sort of mood she would be in when she arrived at work. It was a small company. We would have a brief "stand up" meeting on Monday mornings, with all the staff. If the MD discovered someone had made a mistake or not done something they should have done, she would shout at them and berate them in front of everyone, like a parent would to a child. She seemed to do this especially with the younger employees. Nowadays, we would probably label her behaviour as bullying, but it was different times then. People coped by leaving. We had a very high staff turnover.

Although she never treated me this way as I always stood my ground with her (unlike how I behaved in my personal life, especially in my intimate relationships), it did not make it a good working environment. I found it very uncomfortable witnessing the regular bullying. Also, the workload was excessive. There was other work, in addition to managing the Brazilian city account. It was really a job for two and a half, to three people, but because the clients would not pay more and my boss did not want to lose the accounts, it meant myself and my assistant had to do the best we could.

By now, I had moved to another part of London, having experienced another stressful event at the previous flat. Consequently, I had a three-hour round trip by public transport to the office. I often did this on a Saturday too, working (unpaid) just to try and keep up with all the work. Again, I was rarely alone. It was also part of the culture. I started to resent working so many hours just to try and keep up and even then, never able to complete all of the tasks. Additionally, I missed using my Spanish and I missed Spanish culture. After only six months with the company, I started to look for another job.

I spoke to my contacts at the Spanish Tourist Office in London, but unfortunately, they had no vacancies. Then I discovered the Portuguese Tourist Office in London were seeking a Press and PR Officer. I was unsure if I should go for the job or not, but I had reached the threshold in my current job. I was desperate to leave. Financially though, I could not leave without another job to go to. Even though I had never been to Portugal, and I did not speak Portuguese, my logical, rational mind motivated me to apply, as there was nothing else around at the time. But my heart sank at the thought of it. I still had a feeling that I should be doing something else with my life, something that felt more meaningful to me, especially if I couldn't even use my Spanish. The battle between my head and my heart made me feel so conflicted and in itself was causing me to feel more stressed. My head, as usual, won.

I had assumed the Portuguese PR role was a purely tourism-related one. Nevertheless, I discovered that there was a trade department as well as a tourism department and that, although the main role involved PR for the tourism department, it also included providing PR support for the trade department. It sounded like a great deal of work. I felt concerned about how my time would be divided up. Consequently, in the interview, as the directors of both departments were the ones interviewing me, I asked them. They seemed vague regarding how much time I would be spending with each department. Each director wanted a greater percentage of my time than would be humanely possible! I had a bad feeling about it. It was not a good sign. But, I was seduced by the prestige of the role, the salary, the responsibility, having an office to myself for the very first time and being able to leave my current job with a new one to go to. And so I pushed the niggling concern to the back of my mind and when they offered me the job, I accepted.

After leaving my old job, I had two weeks before starting the next role. At that time, being an extremely responsible and conscientious person, who also cared a great deal about how others perceived me, I organised what used to be referred to as a "busman's holiday" for myself because although I was confident about my skills and experience in the travel industry, and in marketing and PR, I did not want the Portuguese to think I was underqualified for the job, or ignorant, having never been to their country! That was more important to me than having a proper break, restoring and recharging myself. So, instead I armed myself with several guidebooks, swatting up on the country as I travelled around, seeing as much of it as I could in the two weeks. It was not a great deal, but it was enough to make me feel a little better when I started the job.

Something else I had not realised until I started work there, was that the role also included translating particular documents that the trade department would give me, from Portuguese to English! Even though there are similarities between Spanish and Portuguese, I knew I did not have the level of skill required to do that. And so, without giving a second thought to the workload that came with the job, my logical, rational mind that had convinced me to take a "buswoman's holiday" (in my case) prior to starting rather than have a proper break to rest and recharge, motivated me to do an evening course to learn the language. This was not just conversational Portuguese either. It was an A-level in it! I believed I had to make sure it was a high enough level that it would actually enable me to do the translations!

A few weeks after starting, I was already beginning to question my decision to take the job. There was so much to learn about the country itself, the language, and especially the trade aspects, in such a short space of time. I don't remember all the trade products now, but I do remember having to promote the wine (the easy part for me!). But there was also the promotion of their shoes (which I knew little about) and cork (which I knew nothing about!). The directors were aware of this when they hired me and assured me the staff in the department would help me learn. In reality, though, the training was very informal and very brief. At that time, I felt unable to request more training, which I felt I desperately needed, as I was concerned they might, rightly or wrongly, consider me unfit for the role, and I needed the job. There seemed to be no respite in my stress levels, which I had hoped for in changing jobs. I continued to feel stress on an ongoing basis.

I subsequently also discovered that my position had previously been carried out not by one, but by two people working full-time, both Portuguese nationals, who were in the position for years. So, this was yet another example of the "do more with less" culture of the modern era. Additionally, it appeared I had been right to be concerned in the interview with regard to my roles, responsibilities and how my time would be divided, because throughout my time there, the directors never reached an agreement about it. Thus, my colleagues could make use of, or rather make demands on, my time, as they felt they needed to.

Consequently, I found myself at the mercy of those that "shouted the loudest" and were the most forceful – or rather, the ones that triggered the most fear in me! What made it even more difficult was that at the time, although I was confident generally, I was also what could be described as a "people pleaser". I did not like conflict and would do a great deal to avoid it, particularly taking on more work than I should, rather than risk upsetting someone. All these factors made managing my workload incredibly challenging.

In addition, I had to contend with interpersonal issues in the office with one particular member of staff, who had been in their role for years. I was unable to trust them at all, for reasons I won't elaborate on, and I was meant to collaborate with them on a number of projects. It made the already challenging job even more difficult and it added further to the stress and pressure I was experiencing.

Although we had a contract with an outside PR agency to assist me with some of the tourism work, I had to generate the work for them, which then meant more work for me. I felt totally unsupported in my job on so many levels. I felt unable to speak to anyone at work about the problems I was experiencing with the interpersonal issues, or the ever-increasing workload. The two directors took a very "hands off" approach. The only time I had the courage to speak to them, at least about the workload, and my struggle with more time being demanded of me by the trade department than I felt able to give due to all the tourism work, I felt they provided no support at all and they just put the responsibility back on to me.

I would have been overjoyed with this leadership style, and all the autonomy, had I still been in the Canary Island role. This is because the island was small, I knew it and my clients well, spoke the language fluently, had a clearly defined role and responsibilities, had the experience and so on. I would have relished the freedom, the autonomy and confidence they had in me to do the job(s). In contrast, I had none of these positive factors in my role at the Portuguese office. And so I felt their leadership approach really hindered me. I had no mentor, no one to help me develop the skills I needed (mostly with regard to the trade department), to manage the workload, or to resolve the interpersonal issue with my colleague.

Knowing I had opportunities to visit Portugal again as part of the job in the coming months kept me going for a while, as did consuming lots of caffeine and sugar. I ate a chocolate bar daily to boost my energy in the afternoons. Usually, when I got home, the first thing I would do would be to pour myself a glass of wine, then another, eat some crisps with dips, then throw some instant pasta in a pan, and add some readymade sauce. That would be dinner! I was lucky. At the time I had a high metabolism and thus I had no visible signs, such as weight gain, which would have let me know I needed to look at my diet.

On other nights, after a long day at work, I'd go straight out and meet friends for drinks and dinner, or drinks and clubbing, in my attempts to numb out and switch off from the horrendous workload and office challenges. It was affecting my sleep though, especially on the nights when I drank less. It would take me ages to switch off and go to sleep. Then, I'd wake in the middle of the night and find myself thinking of all the things that were on my never-ending work "to-do" list and dreading anyone else adding to it unexpectedly in the day.

Then, in the week of my 30th birthday, I became physically unwell. I thought it was just a bad cold but then it seemed to become more like the flu. I felt so ill that I had to have a couple of days off work, but no-one covered my role(s) and responsibilities when I was not in the office. But, knowing that my already heavy workload was only increasing in my absence and was causing me so much stress and anxiety, I forced myself to go back to work before I had recovered. At the same time, I was experiencing issues in my personal life yet again. I was in a relationship in which I felt more alone when I was with my partner than when I was physically on my own. Nevertheless, I did not have the strength or courage to have the uncomfortable conversation and end it. I felt increasingly unhappy and powerless both at work and in my personal life, and yet still I carried on, pushing myself regardless.

In addition, although I never really enjoyed the trade-related aspects of my job, I even stopped enjoying the tourism aspects, including work trips abroad. The yearning for a job that I felt was more meaningful was growing even stronger too. With this, and my health issues, I started to seriously consider a career change, believing that it would not only give me more meaning in my life, but would also be the solution to reducing my stress and having a manageable workload. This resulted in me applying to (and subsequently becoming accepted on), a full-time degree course in psychology and counselling. It was not due to start until the following September and so I had many months to work up the courage to tell my bosses and to help them find a replacement for me. Moreover, I hoped to find out what was going on with my body and sort that out too. That was the plan!

From chronic stress to burnout
Things began to get worse. I experienced a fear of flying for the first time ever on a short business trip to Portugal for a conference. There was mild turbulence, but I felt terrified. I could not believe my reaction, as I had flown so many times since I started working in the travel industry (and prior to that on holidays). I could not believe how anxious I suddenly became about flying. It did not seem rational, but I felt powerless to stop it.

Additionally, I had continual health problems. The flu seemed to linger on in some form. I was experiencing strange aches and pains, particularly in my muscles, also light and sound sensitivity, certain food sensitivities, and IBS-type symptoms. I was getting more and more tired as time passed too. I did not even feel better after a week's holiday visiting a friend abroad and actually slept through most of it! I had to drag myself out of bed to go to the beach even for just one day. It seemed such a waste of a holiday and was so out of character for me. After the holiday, I was still continuously exhausted. I had moved back in with my parents to save money, which meant a more difficult commute. I started to struggle even just to make the journey into work, let alone be able to do the job and do it effectively.

Along with my strange, ongoing physical symptoms and exhaustion, I even began to feel anxious at work. I dreaded going in. As I sat down in my office each day, I would look at all the work needing my attention and feel overwhelmed. I dreaded turning my computer on and seeing the ever-increasing numbers of emails needing a response from me (mobile phones were still very basic then, without internet access). I dreaded seeing people approaching my office door, or the telephone ringing, as it only meant one thing, more work for me to do! I was so stressed and anxious about the workload and feeling so unsupported, that when the phone did ring, I felt huge waves of anxiety and burst into tears. It was so unlike me. I never cried at work – until now – but I felt unable to control myself and my emotions.

In the past, prior to the chronic stress period and final burnout, correlating with a number of health conditions, I had always considered myself a resilient and self-determined person, as Deci and Ryan (1985) would call it, at least with regard to my work life and career goals. Right from the time when the government grant was not enough to fund my college diploma, I strove to find a way to earn the money to fund myself, as I previously mentioned, and to the time when I wanted to move back to the UK after living and working abroad, I found a creative solution. I was focused, driven and often single-minded in my determination to achieve my goals. But, I felt that part of me slipping away, the more my workload and other issues increased.

I experienced a decreasing sense of ability to cope, physically, mentally and emotionally, and consequently I found myself unable to take constructive action to change my situation at work, and instead was constantly reacting to the situation and events – until I reached "rock bottom". I had never experienced such exhaustion like it in my life, not even when I had glandular fever in my teens. It made me feel quite helpless and powerless.

It began to dawn on me that my plan of a smooth transition to a new career at a point, months off in the future, was no longer viable. I had reached breaking point. I had nothing left to give. I could no longer carry out my job. I could take no more of the chronic stress and exhaustion. No matter what others thought of me, I had to resign. I could not sustain the interpersonal conflict either, and even though I was still afraid, I did not have the energy to continue in my unhappy relationship. So, finally I ended it.

I had thought that finishing my job, and ending my relationship, would see an end to my symptoms and a return to my "normal" self. But, after a few weeks of no improvement, I felt worse mentally, like a dark cloud was hanging over my head which I could not shift. I now recognise I had become depressed, but at the time, I did not realise it, particularly as I had never experienced anything like it before in my life. When I visited my GP, he reported he thought my symptoms were probably a sign of ME, or Chronic Fatigue Syndrome (CFS), as it is more commonly referred to now. There was no actual medical test he could do to find out, rather it was based on the symptoms I described and the duration I had been having them. He could not tell me how long it would be before I would get better, or even if I would get better at all. There was no "magic pill" to cure me. I felt very scared.

(NB: It is possible, and probable, that I had CFS at the time, but I also now know I was suffering from work-related burnout too, as I explained in the Introduction.)

From burnout to recovery
The GP had said there was no treatment for CFS (at that time). Determined to be well enough to achieve my goal of starting the university course in six months' time, and thankfully with some money saved up, I was willing to try anything and everything, no matter how strange it may seem! I read what I could find about CFS (which at the time was also deemed "Yuppie Flu" as it seemed to affect what was described as young, middle-class professionals), nutrition and other topics, when I had the energy, as part of my self-devised healing plan. I had previously contemplated psychotherapy but had been too afraid to try it (again, they were different times). I was now ready. I knew it would not cure my health issues, but I hoped it would help me deal with how it was making me feel and rid me of the dark cloud I felt had been hanging over my head since leaving my job and relationship. I felt a complete loss of identity, now physically being unable to work and earn money, something I had been doing on and off since I was 13. Therapy turned out to be fundamental to my recovery (as I describe in Part One of this book). It helped in so many ways, such as raising my awareness about many aspects of what I was experiencing and facilitating other insights. It also helped me to begin to change my mindset and my behaviour.

Additionally, I watched many episodes of Oprah, which happened to be on television at the time. The guests on her show covered many aspects of what is described as the "mind, body, spirit", or "self-help" movement, which helped me to discover other topics and tools that assisted me in my recovery, such as writing a gratitude journal (see Key 5). I also learnt about the importance of making your heart sing, something which I had neglected in my life for years, in favour of meeting the needs of my rational, logical mind, rather than what my heart and soul needed (as described in Key 5). This resulted in me doing a brief evening course in musical theatre, which despite my continuing energy challenges at the time, I found so uplifting that it boosted my energy.

Other recommendations I read about and tried included alternative treatments, such as Chinese herbal medicine (which I reacted badly to!), kinesiology (which was nice but I did not notice any benefit) and acupuncture (which I was initially scared to try, but which I actually found very relaxing and beneficial!). I also had sessions with a nutritionist and experienced what was at the time perceived as a radical change in diet – no gluten, no sugar, no processed food, no dairy, no caffeine, no chocolate, no alcohol, and so on. I started a regular meditation practice too. I came across a leaflet on reiki, described as a form of "energy healing", so I tried that too. I found reiki so relaxing that I did a couple of short courses to become a reiki practitioner, so I could give reiki to myself and others when I felt able to.

Furthermore, I taught myself to meditate and became very interested in spirituality, and the concept of there being a "universal energy", something larger than myself, and the concept of "oneness", that we are all connected. These concepts gave me a sense of hope that I would recover, which was really important to me, particularly with regard to my mental well-being.

Thankfully, all of these factors, in addition to resting and recharging properly, meant I was well enough to start the degree in psychology and counselling. In the first year, I just focused on getting through the course, and sleeping and resting when not studying. Nevertheless, by the second year, I was feeling considerably better. And so, after giving my then boyfriend a few massages, and hearing him say I was so good at it that I should train in that too, I listened. I also listened to my logical, rational mind, which enjoyed being told I was good at something, and it was something that would then enable me to start earning money again, when qualified. I did not "ask" my body how it felt! I ignored it and pushed myself to do the part-time anatomy and physiology and massage course on top of my degree.

To recover from my health issues, I also had some NLP sessions with an NLP practitioner, which I found very beneficial. The practitioner also ran a 10-month weekend training course in NLP, hypnotherapy and coaching. My by then ex-boyfriend had managed to complete the course along with recovery from CFS and completing the final year of his psychology degree course, and had been able to work straight afterwards, using the tools from the course. Consequently, he suggested I do the course too. So, again, driven by a need to achieve (and feel good enough) rather than considering my body, I listened to my logical rational mind, which said it would qualify me to see clients when I finished, and I could learn more useful personal development tools that I could also apply to myself, and so I embarked on the extra course. Once I started the final year of my degree, I began to find the extra course at the weekends a struggle. Thankfully, I met the man who subsequently became my husband on the course and he gave me the physical and psychological support I needed to get through it, although it was far from easy.

The Second Burnout Cycle

A note about the second burnout cycle

Although this book focuses on work-related stress and burnout, the periods of paid work were fewer in the second cycle than the first. My journey was not straightforward. Unlike the first burnout experience, I did not have periods of continuous full-time work prior to it. Additionally, some of the periods of significant stress were during the time I was completing a doctorate. I have since discovered that there is such a thing as PhD Burnout! Therefore, for ease and flow purposes, I have focused on the work-related aspects as much as possible, but have also included my time on the doctorate and the stress associated with that, as that was implicated in my second burnout too.

Life in balance and a high level of resilience once more

After the courses ended, I had a few months' break during which time I got married, had a honeymoon and moved to the south coast. Then I set myself up in private practice (initially with my husband, and then subsequently on my own as our careers took different directions). I worked with clients, offering sessions from reiki and massage to spiritual counselling and hypnotherapy. Additionally, having had therapy, been part of a self-development group on my degree and done so much work on myself as part of my recovery, I had become passionate about self-development, and helping people raise their self-awareness in particular. Consequently, I ran a weekly personal development group which included guided visualisations and meditation. I continued with my own meditation practice too, as I found it so helpful in managing any stress and raising my self-awareness.

Working for myself in private practice had many benefits including having complete autonomy. I was able to do work that I was fully engaged with. It also afforded me the ability to work the number of hours that I felt were manageable, and it gave me the time to take proper care of my well-being – mentally, emotionally and physically. Although I found it rewarding working with clients and helping them change, I also found it lonely at times, especially not being able to talk to anyone about my work, due to maintaining client confidentiality (I was unaware at this time of the importance of clinical supervision). I missed being part of a team. Moreover, I wanted to help more people to change than I would ever be able to with one-to-one client work or running a personal development group.

I had noticed that my clients often sought help because they had self-esteem issues which were affecting their relationships with others, or even finding a partner. I knew what that was like as I had experienced these issues myself and learnt a great deal from them. This gave me the idea to write a book on the subject to help others learn from my experience, to improve their relationship with themselves and others. The thought of reaching and helping many more people gave me a renewed sense of meaning and purpose in my life. I was bursting with ideas. I felt I had so much to write, and having never done it before, I wanted to dedicate myself full-time to writing the book. And so I wound down my practice and spent the next two years writing 22 Boyfriends to Happiness: My Story and the seven secrets on how to find true love and happiness, which I self-published in 2008.

In my work as a self-publishing writer, I was in complete control. I decided how much time to spend writing each day, when to relax, enjoy life, top up on my creative well. I was very lucky too. My husband had work and was willing to support me. I could not have done it otherwise. The process of writing was not without its challenges though. I did experience the occasional moment of stress, particularly in the beginning, as I overcame psychological hurdles regarding my self-efficacy about writing a book or reflected back on some of the emotionally painful events in my life. Nevertheless, my workload was completely manageable, I had made sure of that, by focusing solely on writing rather than trying to juggle working with clients and writing. I maintained my other well-being practices too, that I had discovered during my recovery, including giving myself reiki, paying for the occasional complementary therapy when we had the money. I also balanced the challenging periods of reflection with time spent doing fun, inexpensive activities, or socialising, that made me feel happy, to cultivate positive emotions and keep my "creative well" topped up.

Some episodes of acute stress but maintaining a good level of resilience

Another period of self-employment

After publishing my book, I set myself up in business again. This time I focused on psychological coaching, specialising in the ideas discussed in my book, helping people improve their relationship with themselves and others, and enhance their well-being. The work included giving talks, running workshops and delivering coaching. I was lucky enough to get involved with The Cottage Healing Centre in Tamworth, Staffordshire. The team, who were all really friendly, were very supportive of me, my book and my work. So, although I still did not have any formal supervision, and all my client work was confidential, I was able to find a support network among the fellow practitioners and the manager at that time. It made a big difference.

The other benefit of being self-employed again was being in complete control of how I spent my time, and the events I chose to attend, and so on. It meant I was able to ensure I maintained a good balance of paid work activities (and unpaid, such as household chores), rest and leisure/socialising (time with my husband, socialising with friends and family and so forth). Additionally, it enabled me to maintain a healthy diet with balanced meals and minimal processed food. I also discovered mindfulness around this time, and after attending a weekend course on it, I began to include it as part of my regular well-being, or resilience, practice.

Nevertheless, I missed aspects of being an employee, particularly the continual income, the teamwork and working normal office hours. I found the unpredictability and uncertainty of self-employment still challenging to deal with too. And even after all the therapy I had had, all the personal development work, and the qualifications I had thus far gained, I continued to have issues with feelings of self-efficacy, that is, feeling good enough with regard to carrying out the role of change facilitator/psychological coach. I was suffering from 'imposter syndrome'.

Inner parts conflict
By this time, it would be less than a year until I turned 40. I found that difficult. It was difficult to accept that, career wise, I was still not where I had hoped I'd be. My logical, rational mind thought that more training, with another qualification, would solve that problem. But, my heart was more interested in Buddhism, especially Buddhist psychology and mindfulness. Consequently, I researched mindfulness courses and discovered that Bangor University offer a Masters in the subject. I read the course programme and it sounded wonderful. It made my heart sing and I was very excited about it.

But, my logical, rational mind was against that idea! It noted I would be 45 by the time I graduated the five-year course. It said it would mean starting over yet again, once I qualified. My rational mind thought, irrespective of how interested I was in it, that other people would NOT be interested in being taught mindfulness and therefore, I would not be able to make a living out of it! How wrong that part of me was then, as demonstrated by the boom in mindfulness that subsequently followed! My rational mind suggested that as I have a degree in psychology, and years of experience working in organisations, I should consider doing a master's in occupational psychology. My mind is impatient and likes me to do things quickly. It said this master's would only take one year (full-time) and I could earn a living from it! It made sense. I did look into it, but it was not for me. There was not enough on the course that actually involved helping people change, which is what I am passionate about. I kept searching.

Totally unaware at the time of the prevalence of burnout in the healthcare profession, particularly compared to other professions, I also thought about working in the NHS. My mind said it would enable me to help a wider variety of people and satisfy the part of me that enjoyed being an employee and part of a team. However, at that time, the rules for working as a psychologist in the NHS were changing. A doctorate would now be required. My mind was very excited about the prospect of having a doctorate in counselling psychology. It was the area of psychology I was most interested in, because I value helping others change and it would expand on what I'd studied on my undergraduate degree. I hoped it would finally enable me to feel good enough at my second career too.

Nevertheless, another part of me was very concerned about the amount of work it would involve. A person I knew who had recently completed a PhD warned me that a doctorate is incredibly demanding and that they hardly saw their family or friends during it, due to the high workload! I felt a pang of fear deep down in the pit of my stomach as I heard this. But, just as I had done in the interview for the Portuguese PR job ten years previously, I allowed my mind to push the fearful feeling out of my awareness. I told myself I knew how to take care of myself properly now – mentally, emotionally and physically – unlike before the first burnout. To further assuage the part of me that was concerned, I found out as much information as possible prior to starting, to try and ascertain if I could manage the workload and the potential stress. I thought I had sufficient knowledge, and the skills and so on, to maintain my resilience levels to cope effectively with the high workload and stress during the three-year, full-time course. At first, I did, but later, I did not.

The first year of the doctorate
I found the first year challenging with regard to returning to studying after a number of years away from it, but the university provided us with a good level of support, both in relation to the academic aspects, but also with the practitioner aspect – by finding us suitable work placements and supporting us in that area.

My first work placement was within a local NHS service. They had just started to run a pilot primary care mental health service, along the lines of what later developed into the Improving Access to Psychological Therapies (IAPT) service. The service, as the name suggests, was established to increase the access to psychological therapy, in other words, to make it more easily accessible on the NHS than it had been traditionally. This was to help the growing number of people who were signed off from work, or unable to work, due to experiencing mild anxiety and/or depression, to return to, or be able to, work. The psychiatric nurses who had been tasked with providing the counselling for this service openly expressed their appreciation to me for joining them, as they felt ill-prepared for the task, given they had no counselling training at all. It felt great to be appreciated and supported.

At the time, GPs referred to us clients who they thought met the criteria. Sometimes at assessment or during therapy, I discovered a client had more complex mental health issues, a history of trauma or abuse for example, that perhaps they had not shared with their GP, and I felt they needed more longer-term therapy instead. I would discuss this with my clinical supervisor, who was a fantastic support, and our values were highly aligned. When it was appropriate, we were able to refer the client on to our Secondary Care service, for clients with more complex mental health issues. Although not perfect, the system worked reasonably well, given the available resources. The work was very rewarding, and the workload felt manageable. I felt happy working for the service and very supported.

But, an organisational (university) stressor I had not been aware of at the start, was that we had to accrue a specific number of client therapy hours each year of the course in order to pass. So, even if I ensured I attended each session to deliver therapy to my clients, sometimes, as I discovered, they did not turn up, for a variety of reasons. We were also required to submit a certain number of client therapy case studies each year. Again, this meant being reliant on finding a client who was willing to be a case study and then relying on them to attend all the sessions that were necessary, in order to fulfil the requirements of the case study. I found the uncertainty and unpredictability of this aspect stressful, particularly as all I could do was do my best with regard to delivering therapy, and the rest was in the client's control.

In addition to attending lectures, completing essays and delivering therapy, and more, we also had to complete a research thesis by the end of the course. The deadline for submitting our research idea was at the end of the first year. The research would then be carried out in the second year, with final submission in the third year. However, my stress-management strategy meant I planned well ahead and started everything earlier. My logical mind convinced me that if I started it all sooner, it would give me a buffer, in case of any unforeseen issues.

By the end of the first year of the course I was starting to feel very tired again, as the episodes of acute stress had been increasing, along with the workload. I sought advice from a health practitioner. She told me I should reduce my stress levels and relax more! My mind told me I could not afford to listen to my body's needs and heed her advice, if I were to keep on top of the workload, get ahead with the research and achieve my goal (i.e. pass the doctorate).

Therefore, rather than most of my peers who took the summer off, recharging and enjoying themselves, I mostly read, planned and worked on the early stages of my thesis! The action that I did take to help myself though was to commit to doing an hour's meditation upon waking, as many days a week as possible. I also avoided all non-essential social engagements, so that I could get rest when I was not working.

From acute stress to chronic stress and decreasing levels of resilience

The second year of the doctorate
In order to obtain as much experience as possible during the course, we were encouraged to change work placements each year. The university did not provide work placement support beyond the first year. I was lucky enough to be able to remain in the same NHS Trust,

and begin working in their Secondary Care mental health service. This service provided longer-term therapy for clients with more complex mental health issues, such as bi-polar disorder, OCD, or multiple mental health issues, for example. This also meant a change of clinical supervisor. Although my supervisor was very personable and likeable, I experienced a clash of values with him from the start. Suffice it to say that although I felt professionally supported by him, I did not feel personally supported. Unlike in my role in the Portuguese PR job, having developed personally and professionally since then, I did directly address these challenges with my supervisor and effectively managed them, but I still found it stressful.

There were fewer lectures to attend in the second year, which was a relief, but there was much more work to do with regard to the doctoral thesis. Like many doctoral students, I struggled to recruit participants from within the university and had to extend my search beyond it. Therefore, I had to travel from one end of the country to the other and so it took so much longer to complete all the interviews than I had ever anticipated. Additionally, transcribing all the interviews also took much longer than I expected. These delays meant I was unable to stick to my planned schedule with regard to analysing the interviews and the stress was ongoing.

Another factor at this time was that we had moved to the Midlands as my husband had a contract with a company in the region, which subsequently ended six months later, and he could not find work in the area, which we both found stressful. Eventually, he secured a contract, but it meant him working away from home. I felt quite alone as my family are all based near London. Furthermore, with Mark working away, I had trouble sleeping, having been the victim of crime twice when living in London. I was also struggling to find the time and energy to maintain a healthy diet and found myself resorting to my old "crutches" to keep me going – sugary foods, chocolate and some wine!

I began to feel emotionally, and physically, that I needed more support. A part of me yearned to be nearer my family, and my husband and I felt that we should relocate, even though I still had the course to complete. My logical mind was against it as I still had lectures to attend and the NHS work placement to complete, which would be difficult if we moved. I felt trapped and helpless to give myself what I felt I needed. Then, suddenly, it was as though the decision was made for me.

We got home one night (thankfully Mark had come home for the weekend) to find that we had been burgled! It brought the previous crimes flooding back and I burst into tears. That night we stayed in a local hotel and discussed the possibility of relocating. I was so stressed and tired that I did not have the resilience to cope with staying living in the Midlands on my own, whilst Mark worked away, after that. So less than three weeks later we moved to Surrey, near my parents and five minutes from where my husband was working. And then, two weeks later, my husband was told his contract would be terminated at the end of the month! It was yet another stressor. At this point, I had completed the second university year, but I still had two months of the NHS work placement remaining. This meant I had a total of seven hours of travelling (minimum), by train each week to the Midlands, until my contract ended. I found it stressful and very tiring.

At the same time, I also had to find a new work placement (which is an unpaid position) for my third year. This proved more difficult now that we had moved to a different region. The pressure was on to find the final work placement fast, to ensure I had enough time to accrue the required number of clinical hours by the end of the third year. I emailed and telephoned countless services trying to find a work placement. In the end, I managed to actually secure two placements, one in an NHS IAPT service and another delivering therapy for an addiction treatment charity.

Additionally, instead of taking time off to rest and recharge before the third and final year, I still had to work on my research thesis. I felt under huge pressure and was fearful I would not have enough time to complete the data analysis process of it, once the new term, and the new placements, started. I could not see how I would fit it in on top everything else. I felt I needed to try and do as much as I could during the university summer break to keep up. So, I resorted to my old, negative habit of pushing through, and kept going. I should have listened to my body, which was exhausted, and taken a proper break instead.

A diary entry at this time:

> *What I've noticed is that I have a fear of taking time now, to rest and recharge. I haven't achieved any of my July goals and I feel almost panicky at the thought of taking a few days*

off to recharge. My 'to do' list is already so long and I feel I've got pressing things to do before my meeting with my research supervisor next week, so that's a 'no' to time off this weekend...Then next weekend, I will be needing to write up the notes from the meeting and that will further add to the original 'to do' list/goals. What a cycle! So, even though there was a delay in starting [the analysis process, due to the difficulties in recruiting participants] I am aware, I still expect myself to finish at least a key aspect of the research work, in September!

A part of me felt such a need to escape, to rest, recharge and relax and have some fun. I told myself that if I had a holiday booked, to look forward to, I would be able to work more quickly and be more focused. Therefore, one of the methods I used to cope was distraction. I found myself surfing the internet, looking at holiday destinations and thinking of where we might go, if Mark was able to find a contract to start after it. But the distraction was not a productive use of my time. We did take a short holiday abroad (thanks to the credit card!), but it was not enough to restore me.

I also attempted to reduce my stress by taking other practical action. This included researching the possibility of transferring to a university nearer to me for the final year, but to no avail. If I transferred, I would have to start all over again. I could not contemplate dropping out either. I had, I thought, only one year remaining. I had come too far, there were too many "sunk costs" for me to do that. And so, I struggled on.

The third year of the doctorate
I was excited to start working in the NHS IAPT placement, as working for the NHS as a counselling psychologist continued to be my ultimate aim. The service where the therapy would be delivered, and the office, was located within a small hospital. This meant it was only a short walk through the hospital to the clinic rooms from the office, which was similar to the other NHS service I had worked in. This time-saving factor was a great help for many reasons, but particularly if a client cancelled it meant I could return to the office and catch up on other work. The other similarity was that I was part of a small team. We all got on well together. The manager (also my clinical supervisor) had values that were aligned with my own thankfully, and so I experienced her as really supportive and appreciative of the therapeutic work I was doing with clients.

There was a totally different organisational set-up with regard to my other work placement with an addiction/substance misuse charity. It was a much smaller organisation and the team running the department I worked in was very small. Although the team, including the manager, knew a great deal about working with addictions, and were experienced working with clients in this field, they were not trained counsellors or psychologists. Hence I, along with the other volunteer part-time counsellors (who came in different days to me) provided the therapy services. Therefore, they were not able to provide me with clinical supervision. I had to seek it externally and pay for the sessions, which meant I only had one session a month. I got on well with the team and I certainly felt they were supportive personally. Nevertheless, I was new to working in the area of addictions and so professionally I felt I needed more support, but it was not available.

I experienced a further stressor in my third year relating to my doctoral thesis. Each doctoral student was meant to have two research supervisors to support them, ideally both employed by the university. I was only able to find one supervisor. I had to search outside the university for the other and was lucky enough to find Professor Tim Carey, who was willing to take on the role, in addition to his many other responsibilities at his own university. Then, my internal supervisor left! Professor Carey did what he could via email to supervise me, as he was by now based in Australia. It took months for our university to employ someone. Subsequently, I was without internal supervision support until some way into the second term of the third year. This was another factor that added to the stress I was experiencing.

Even though I only had to attend university once a week in the third year, it meant travelling up to the Midlands from Surrey the day before so that I could be there in time for the morning lecture. After a full day at university, I always found the long journey home gruelling. It also meant I got home late in the evening, which then made me tired the following day! Unfortunately, I increasingly resorted to my old coping mechanisms to manage my stress and mounting tiredness, consuming sugary foods and chocolate on a regular basis, which is something I had not done in years. I also started to drink wine more frequently, which again, I had not done to such an extent in many years after committing to take proper care of myself. My behaviour should have been a warning sign to me,

97

signalling it was time for me to stop and give myself what I really needed, rather than to continue trying to push through using artificial energy enhancers.

Even though I was still doing some meditation and mindfulness, which I consider my daily prevention "medicine", I found myself unable to do it often enough to restore my resilience levels. I lacked the energy to get up sufficiently early to do it before work on my placement days, or on the day I had to travel to or from university. I only really felt able to do it at weekends, which was not enough for my stressed mind and depleted body.

I was having weekly therapy sessions, a requirement of the course. I found it helpful to unburden myself to my therapist about how I was feeling mentally, emotionally and physically, about the doctorate, all my stressors and my increasing tiredness. My therapist encouraged me to see my GP. I was very concerned about my ability to keep going and complete the doctorate, and actually wanted some external validation that I did need to do something to avoid another burnout, and so I took her advice. The GP gave me a letter for the university.

He wrote:

> Mrs Buchan is suffering from fatigue. Though she is able to work, I do not think she is able to continue at the level and pace she may have completed previously. I believe it may be up to six months before Mrs Buchan is capable of working at full capacity.

I experienced an inner conflict hearing the GP's response. A part of me felt relieved to have confirmation from a professional that something had to change, that I could not continue as I was. That part felt relieved I had been given legitimate permission to breathe and to slow down. This permission was something, for some reason, in spite of having already experienced burnout, I had not felt able to give myself. It would mean though instead of finishing the doctorate in three years, it would take me four. Consequently, another part of me felt disappointed and low. This was the part of me eager to finish it and move on to what I set out to achieve, working for the NHS as a counselling psychologist.

The fourth year of the doctorate
I felt somewhat relieved that, having finished all my other university work and clinical work, I was able to focus solely on finishing the

research thesis and the doctorate portfolio. This meant that I was working from home too, with only occasional visits to the Midlands to attend meetings with my internal research supervisor. It was a relief to not have to travel so much, or multi-task so much. However, I found working solely on the doctoral thesis came with other challenges. I experienced a sense of isolation, not being able to meet up with my fellow students, who were all busy with work, studying and/or family life. I missed their support. I felt a need for more support from the university too, particularly as, unlike my peers who had two supervisors paid for by the university to support them, I was still reliant on the external supervisor (Professor Carey), and his good will, for the secondary supervision.

Additionally, although my mind was enjoying the research as that part of me relishes a challenge, loves learning and immersing myself in a subject, my heart was not in it due to the subject matter. I had, in my quest to minimise my stress levels, focused on where I could find a gap in the research as quickly as possible. This ended up being the subject of psychological change, specifically men's experience of this. But, my heart had wanted to find a subject it would find engaging, that it would be passionate about. I had wanted to study mindfulness, but I could not find a gap in the literature that I could contribute to, that would also be related to the counselling psychology profession – not in the time I had to meet the submission deadline. And so, my head won, and I went with the topic of psychological change. Therefore, and especially without the fulfilling aspect of delivering therapy, my levels of engagement, along with my level of resilience, were rapidly decreasing.

Post-graduation and another inner conflict

Finally, in July, I graduated. I felt so proud of my achievement. I had not only become the first person in our family to go to university, but also to obtain a doctorate. It made all the struggle seem worthwhile, at least to my mind. But, after the celebrations – a lovely meal with my family and then a wonderful afternoon tea in central London with my husband, I suddenly felt a huge void. My life had been so full for the previous four years that I had not had time for anything but the doctorate – now what? What was next? My body (heart and soul too!) said – relax, rest, have fun, go with the flow and see what happens! My driven to achieve, perfectionistic mind had other ideas.

I had hoped to be employed as a counselling psychologist in the NHS directly after the doctorate but there were no such posts available.

There were jobs available within an NHS IAPT service I had previously worked in, but the positions were for High Intensity (HI) therapists (which did not require a doctorate). In addition to delivering therapy, attending meetings, clinical supervision and other NHS related activities, the role included an intensive training programme of Cognitive Behavioural Therapy (CBT), the treatment of choice in IAPT, which involved attending university two days a week, and completing assignments and case studies.

My mind said apply. I was desperate to be an employee again, to receive a regular income, and be part of a team. I was desperate to use my skills helping people change too. I had also discovered that if I wanted to work in the NHS, which had always been the goal, I would need to be good at delivering CBT. Although the training on the doctorate did include some CBT, it was quite basic. I felt ill-equipped for a full-time role in the NHS which predominantly relied on using CBT therapy. A part of me believed that unless I did the further CBT training, I would not be good enough to work in the NHS now, even with a doctorate! My mind also rationalised that the post was only for one year. After that, I would have the training and qualification in CBT I needed and would then have more options available to me. To my logical mind, it seemed a great deal more manageable than the doctorate. How could I not apply?

Another part of me did not want to apply for the role at all. This part of me, aside from wanting a complete rest, and especially a break from studying, as mentioned, did not want me to spend time and energy improving my knowledge and skills regarding CBT. The thought of it made my heart sink! Although I had had some positive experiences using CBT with clients previously, these were less than those that I had with other more humanistic therapies. I went backwards and forwards constantly asking myself, should I do it or not? I asked other people for their input too about what to do! I felt I was lucky in some respects, that I even had this choice to make about whether to apply for the job or not, and that was only because my husband was in well-paid work at the time. But it was making me feel stressed and drained further, from the constant back and forth over the decision. I felt so stuck.

My mind, the continual dominant force, was still driven to achieve, irrespective of the cost to my health. In contrast, my heart, soul and body wanted me to take some time to appreciate the great accomplishment I had already achieved, to savour the moment and to take a break. This part(s) wanted me to restore my body, to have some fun and relaxation and spend time with my family, friends and our lovely new rescue dog, Tommy. I felt so conflicted, and concerned about my increasing tiredness, I returned to see one of the practitioners (with numerous qualifications including in nutrition and psychotherapy) who had been a great help in my recovery from the first burnout.

I went to her for nutrition advice and for an adrenal gland test, to help me know the impact of stress on my body. The results were not good. Apparently, I was in the "red zone", meaning I was in a chronically stressed state, close to burning out again! I thought I had probably been in that "state" since the time I last visited the GP and got the letter. I shared my dilemma with her, telling her a part of me really wanted to take this NHS job, but I was fearful of my health, especially given what she had told me about my adrenal glands. She is a straight talker – something I value about her. Her response to me was:

> *"Catherine...you have just completed a doctorate. You could do anything you want to do. Why on earth are you even thinking about taking on this job?"*

She had a point! I was over-qualified (except in my mind, with regard to the CBT aspect). She advised me to take a break, recharge my batteries and figure out what I really wanted to do. I thought about what she said. I felt scared about my health and what taking the job could mean for my well-being. But, I also felt scared to face the void, the meaninglessness I felt when I did not have a goal to aim for or a job, and the unknown and the uncertainty. If I did not take the job, then what would I do? What if this was my one chance to get a job in the NHS? What if there were no more counselling psychologist jobs in the NHS anymore? In the end, I did not listen to the practitioner, my husband, who almost begged me not to take the job for fear of what it might do to me, or my heart, body or soul. Instead, I listened to my loud, dominant, logical mind that convinced me it would be all right as it was only for one year.

As is well documented, the 2007/8 financial crisis had a negative impact on the NHS, including the mental health services. By the time I started the NHS IAPT role, many services had been severely reduced, including the Secondary Care mental health services, and some within social care had been cut altogether. This meant the IAPT service I was working in became a "catch all" for many people who needed some form of help or support, even for those the service was not designed for or appropriate for, as the GPs had nowhere else to send them now. Consequently, we were seeing clients with more enduring or complex, mental health issues who needed long-term therapy, which we were unable to give them as we could only provide a limited number of sessions. Some had been receiving social support from a day centre, for example, which offered activities for those experiencing some form of mental health issue but who did not want, or feel able to have, therapy for various reasons. When that service was closed, they were then sent to the IAPT service, where we could not provide what they actually needed. I found these organisational factors very difficult to deal with. I began to experience a clash of values from very early on in the role.

At the end of therapy, some clients needed further sessions, due to having more than one mental health issue, for example. All we could do was discharge them at the end of therapy and inform them that if they felt they needed further treatment, they could contact the service again, but they would have to go back on the waiting list. I also had to inform them I could not guarantee I would be their therapist, which was particularly frustrating for both myself and the client, when we had developed a good therapeutic relationship and they had been making progress.

I felt my schedule was beginning to have a negative impact not only on me, but on my clients too, as I found it so intense. On clinic days, I would arrive at the head office at 7.30 am to ensure I managed to get a parking space, access to a computer, and access to the photocopier, to prepare all my CBT sessions for the day (delivering CBT within IAPT means a great deal of paperwork – at least it did then!). I would grab a coffee and try and rapidly eat a sandwich as I worked, having not had time before I left home to eat breakfast. I would subsequently pack up all my work and drive to the GP surgery, where I would deliver therapy. I would have back-to-back sessions, unless someone cancelled, then drive the 40 to 60 minutes home, depending on traffic, unpack from that day and re-pack for the next day.

This was further compounded, I felt, by the intensity of the training course. I found it was such a struggle trying to remember all the information we were learning and needed to deliver CBT effectively. I subsequently discovered that the course was originally 18-months long when it started a few years previously. But, I think for budgetary reasons, they reduced the time, but not the workload, so that it could be delivered and completed within a one-year contract. So, once more, it seemed I was in a situation of being expected to achieve the impossible and do more with less!

What also started to feel soul destroying was the lack of appreciation for what was important to me, that is, my values as a humanistic counselling psychologist and my belief that we can only help others to the extent that we have worked on ourselves. I had spent years, and a great deal of money, on personal development, including therapy, and professional development, studying a variety of therapeutic models, developing skills, gaining experience in delivering these different forms of therapy in different contexts, and experiencing success with these with my clients. Therefore, when I started the job, I felt I knew who I was, what my values were, what I stood for. I felt proud of myself too, having successfully completed the doctorate.

But I experienced a lack of appreciation for all of the above factors in relation to helping clients overcome their issues. Instead, all that was appreciated and valued was our ability to understand the list of mental health disorders we had been studying and our ability to effectively deliver the manualised treatment approaches. This is a "one-size fits all" approach to therapy. Consequently, it did not matter if the client had had CBT previously and not found it helpful, or if they felt put off by the use of paper tools, such as thought records, or if they just needed to spend the session being listened to and understood. All that appeared to matter was delivering the evidence-based therapy according to the manual, irrespective of the client's needs or capabilities.

As a psychologist, I fully appreciate the value in this too, of course, particularly for a system that is heavily in demand but insufficiently resourced, as the NHS is. Still, I personally found it conflicted with my own, more humanistic values. As my time in the role, and as the training went on, the more it was "eating away" at my soul. I now recognise that I was experiencing all three components of what the World Health Organization describes as burnout, not only the elements of exhaustion and "reduced personal efficacy", but the "feelings of negativism or cynicism" too (WHO, 2019). Not only that, but I now also perceive that the burnout I was experiencing was, in part at least, due to "an existential deficiency" (Arman et al., 2011), due to the clash of values I was experiencing, as I explain further in Part One of this book (see Key 3).

One of the things that helped me to manage my stress was meditation. However, I had stopped meditating or doing any mindfulness as I felt I could not make the time for it, except for a few snatched minutes at the GP's surgery if a client cancelled, or was running late (and if I didn't have other work to catch up on, which was rare). I was not sleeping well either, and so I felt unable to get up any earlier to meditate, and I was too tired by the time I got home to do it.

Moreover, I was again relying on sugar and caffeine to get myself through the day. However, after being the same weight for years due to my thankfully high metabolism, I found that I was putting on weight and had actually gone up almost two dress sizes! I was becoming increasingly exhausted, depleted of energy, and was dragging myself through each day, wondering how on earth I was going to be able to continue until my contract ended. My body, heart (and soul), and my husband, wanted me to quit my job. But, once more, my mind, rationalising that there was less than a year remaining, and that I had still more learning to complete, that I was not good enough yet, convinced me to continue. It appeared history was repeating itself.

From chronic stress to burnout again
In my struggle, I visited my GP. I was afraid I would end up not being able to work again, and experience other health-related issues as before. I knew something had to give. The GP reported I was unable to sustain my current working levels due to my exhaustion and that I needed longer to complete the course work. Thankfully, I had a great, very understanding manager. She permitted me to have a day a week at home to work on my course work and do admin. I was also given permission not to attend all of the work-related meetings, only the essentials and the compulsory training days. I was given some extra time to complete the course work too. It helped to some extent. It enabled me to persevere, and push through, until the end.

A few weeks before my contract ended, as I was winding down my client work, my manager asked if I wanted to apply for one of the positions they had available. This would be to continue the work I had been doing as an HI therapist, not as a counselling psychologist. A part of me would have loved to have continued working there as my manager was great and we had a really good, supportive team of people. However, I feared my body and soul (and by then my mind too) could not take any more. I knew by then that I needed a break from work and a proper rest, so I declined. Even so, I thought all I needed was to finish my job and have a few months off. Then, I would be ready to return to full-time work in January, three months later. Nevertheless, once my contract ended, I quickly realised and had to accept that that was not going to happen. An extract from my diary at that time reflects the effects of this burnout on me. It is partly why I want to help others to try and avoid the same experience I went through:

> *As I write this, I don't feel ready to face this...the stark reality that I'm not going to have my life back just yet...or the relationship with myself, my husband, my friends – and reconnect with what I love to do, or find out where I fit now, after all the studying...that there is still more to go...and yet, I fear time is running out [I am getting older!]. I have to face up to my limited energy and put a halt to pushing through...Now what? Now, who am I? I fear facing the dramatic changes I believe and suspect I need to make [with regards] to how I live my life, how I am in the world, if I am to really be well again and recover [from burnout].*

From burnout to recovery once more
It is more of a challenge to write about recovery from the second burnout in such a manner that it may still be interesting and also useful to the reader. The first recovery was easier to write about because I had a specific goal I was aiming for from the beginning, to recover enough to start the undergraduate degree. Then I had other experiences or events during the whole recovery period which were very significant and memorable, such as having therapy for the first time, discovering spirituality, teaching myself to meditate, beginning a new relationship and training to be a massage therapist for example. I experienced a whole paradigm shift during that time, which obviously had a dramatic impact on me. Also, I was younger and recovered in a shorter period of time (two and a half years).

In contrast, the second recovery, though as important, was perhaps less dramatic, with fewer standout events or experiences. It took longer (just over four years) too, as I explain later. Therefore, I mainly summarise the process, and include a few memorable events and journal entries. Further details are also included in Part One of this book.

Part of the reason I believe it took longer to recover was that I consciously chose to avoid putting myself under any pressure. So, as I took charge once again of my well-being, I avoided setting myself goals, aside from the goal of recovery and having more balance in my life. This included reflecting on the last few years and working out how I had reached the point I had again. I wanted to ensure I learnt the lessons fully this time, and worked on my workaholic and perfectionistic tendencies, so that I would not burn out again (as I describe in Key 4). I knew I had to restore myself not only physically, but also emotionally and psychologically. I knew I had to reconnect with myself and repair my soul. This was not a straightforward process. I still had to contend with my dominant mind which was, as always, focused on me finding work, generating an income, as soon as possible.

During the first year of this recovery journey, I wanted to return to my mindfulness and meditation practice, having neglected it for too long. And so, when I discovered there was a Mindfulness at Work conference on the week after my NHS contract finished in September 2014, I decided to attend, hoping to reconnect to the part of me that experienced great benefit from it, and wanted to do more regarding teaching it to others. However, my mind was even resistant to that initially and more so than before doing the doctorate, as is demonstrated in this extract from my journal:

> *Attended the Mindfulness at Work conference. I realised I have been in a rush to get rid of all my IAPT notes, to move on and start to rest, recover, start [get back to] mindfulness! I think what it demonstrates in me, is how I live my life and [how I address] my problem[s], rushing to get the discomfort over with and the stress, so I can get to peace and joy! I realised how much I really need to live and breathe mindfulness, for me personally, and a part of me is eager to get back into it, and fully embrace it this time, not just "dabble". However, I know I have a great deal of resistance to living mindfully. My thoughts, from [this] part are:*
> *It's boring!*
> *It slows me down, so I won't achieve much in a day*
> *It makes me feel old, older, if I am going at a slower pace!*

*I will miss the hit of adrenaline from rushing, pressure,
stress.
Where will I get my hit/kicks from, especially as I'm giving
up drinking alcohol and eating sugar again soon!?
Life will be dull and not fun
It is too fluffy and spiritual it seems to me – give me "hard
science" [instead]!*

We were living in a flat at the time. I was being disturbed each night, being a light sleeper anyway, by the neighbours. So, instead of getting up to meditate, I ended up staying in bed longer to catch up on missed sleep. It was a vicious cycle I could not seem to break and so we took the decision to move to a bungalow in a quieter area. Around this time, I turned to psychotherapy again to help me with my recovery, and particularly with the part of me that kept driving me to achieve, to work, to try and be perfect. I had several sessions with a male therapist who I chose because I liked the model of therapy he practised, he was easy to get to by public transport (so that I did not have the stress of driving and finding parking!) and who had availability. Nevertheless, I stopped after six sessions as I felt he did not really understand me and my issue and what I needed, even though I expressed everything. It was frustrating. Money was also a factor, as I was not working.

After two months of living in the new place, our landlord, totally out of the blue, told us he wanted his property back as he wanted to move in. It was so unexpected that I found it stressful to deal with as I did not want to move again. I had reached threshold point with regard to tolerating landlords being in control of my/our lives in this way and told my husband that we needed to find a way to be able to buy a property, so that we had some sense of security and stability. The only way we could afford this was to move in with my parents, but they had no room in the house, so we ended up living in their "summer house" (a wooden shed really), for three months. Luckily Mark had work which took him abroad during that time. I, on the other hand, spent most days in my parents' living room. It was a very challenging time for me, because although I had (and have) a good relationship with my family, it was not conducive to doing the deep reflective work or processing I needed to do on myself. I had been seeing a practitioner for help with my nutrition and physical well-being again but, living with my parents and sharing a small kitchen was not conducive to me sticking to my healing diet either. Thus, my recovery got delayed.

In September 2015, at the start of the second year of recovery, we were still living with my parents. Mark's work continued to take him abroad. I was searching for our new home and thinking about what to do workwise too. Although I felt unable to do deep personal work on myself then, I did feel able to some Continuing Professional Development (CPD), which I needed to do if I was to work as a counselling psychologist delivering therapy still, which my mind wanted me to do. I chose to attend a short course to train in Acceptance and Commitment Therapy (ACT) that autumn. It was wonderful to connect again with something that my heart enjoyed more as, unlike traditional CBT, ACT incorporates elements of Buddhism, which I have been drawn to for many years, including mindfulness. We used ourselves as "clients" on the course to practise and I also found it helpful in terms of my recovery, to apply ACT to myself.

I also made time to reconnect with some of my friends as it was easier from London and I felt I had the energy to do that too. My focus then shifted to moving to a new house and at the start of 2016, we relocated to the south coast. Once I felt settled and recovered from the stress of the previous few months, I started on my personal development and burnout recovery in earnest. This meant returning to the diet I had been recommended by my latest alternative practitioner. It included much journaling and reflecting and "soul searching", trying to re-discover my heart-felt values too. I managed to return to a regular mindfulness practice and spent time in longer periods of meditation. Additionally, I made the most of our new location by the sea and took long walks with our dog Tommy, or on my own, to reconnect with nature, something I had been missing deeply.

However, in spite of this, I had to once again contend with the part of me that, as soon as it saw an opportunity (i.e. in this case, that we were settled now), it would urge me to get back out to work, irrespective of how I was feeling. It wanted me to hurry up and either search for jobs in the NHS or set myself up in private practice. The other part of me urged me to ignore that aspect of me, as it warned me that following its advice would not make me happy, and instead would trigger the workaholic pattern again, which would negatively impact my well-being.

My logical rational mind won briefly, as I found myself pursuing the possibility to present my doctoral research, which investigated men's experience of psychological change, at the annual Male Psychology Conference in London, taking place in June that year. My mind convinced me it was an opportunity I could not afford to miss, even though my heart was not in it. In order to make the most of the conference, and the marketing opportunities too, my logical mind convinced me to create a website, offering my services. But, as soon as the conference was over and I realised I was still feeling burnt out, I was able to listen to my heart and soul, close down the website and once again, return to focusing on doing the deeper processing I needed to do to recover and "find myself" again.

A few months later, September was upon us and the third year of my recovery journey began. As part of my commitment to restoring my well-being, I chose to do another eight-week Mindfulness Based Stress Reduction (MBSR) course. I wanted to do it not only for my own personal interest and benefit, but with a view to also doing further training in it at some point, when I felt recovered enough. During that winter and the following spring, I also continued journaling, meditating and practising mindfulness regularly. I continued to invest time in making my heart sing, spending time in places that helped restore me, in nature and also other places that made me feel connected spiritually. I returned to reading books that inspired me and watched films or programmes that inspired me and that I found uplifting. An entry in my journal demonstrates that I was finally beginning to make some real progress in my recovery: -

> *Walked for an hour. It was lovely, quiet, sunny, soulful. I had an emotional release as I walked, for the long "Dark Night of the Soul", I feel I've been going through all the years of struggle...our financial struggles, my struggle at university with all the workload, and the research and then IAPT...I felt I've reached the threshold of struggle – and now I'm embracing   [ease],   health...loving-compassion, powerfulness...love...I felt nature, the sand, the sea... healing my soul, washing away all the pain of the struggle, the frustration...*

Although I did have thoughts of work and what I should do when I was well enough during the third year of my recovery, they were brief, and I remained focused on restoring my well-being. Nonetheless, I had perceived (or at least been telling myself) that I was still part of the healthcare profession with the aim of returning to delivering psychological therapy at some point. But, that summer, as I was walking along our local beach one morning, it suddenly dawned on me that I had to let go of my goal of returning to the healthcare profession and the hope of working for the NHS as a counselling psychologist. Despite all the time, the money, the training and the years of hard work, I had to let it go. I realised I had to accept that I cannot be a part of the NHS system as it was damaging to my mind, body and soul. I had to accept that even delivering psychological therapy was no longer right for me due to what it requires if you work privately rather than in the NHS.

I had to let it all go, for the sake of my well-being and happiness. I had to leave yet another career in order to fully recover. It was one of the hardest things I have done in my life. I went through a grieving process. I journaled for many pages and I cried many tears. I did other processes. I drew on my mindfulness practices, practising forgiveness, compassion and acceptance. I spent time in nature. At least this time I also knew all the years of training and experience, and my knowledge and skills, were not a complete waste. I would find another way to be able to make use of them but in a different context and in a way that was still aligned with my heart-felt core values, and thus conducive to my well-being and happiness. Even so, it was still an incredibly difficult part of the recovery journey for me personally.

A number of months after that, in September 2017, I entered the fourth year of recovering from burnout. At the start of it, a new opportunity presented itself when my husband, having left his previous employment, set up an organisational coaching and consulting business and asked me if I wanted to be a part of it, which I did. This is because he had been such a support to me over the years and he totally understood that I was still recovering from burnout but was doing much better (as the diary entry below reveals). He was happy for me to work flexibly too. Although my official title was (and is) "co-director", he was also happy for me to take a more supportive role, providing him with coaching supervision, and being a sounding board with regard to his consultancy, as well as doing other tasks such as admin and marketing.

Diary entry:

> *I feel more able than I have in a long time to work. I feel my mental energy is getting much better, for short spaces of time. My physical energy has improved too...although I still need a siesta [most days].*

In addition to feeling well-enough to do some part-time work, I remained committed to fully restoring my well-being, which included making my heart sing. And so that autumn I reconnected with my love of writing and did a creative writing course at the local adult college. This course I did just for the fun of it and to learn something that was not too taxing mentally. It was nice meeting new people too, as we were still relatively new to the area.

As the months passed, I continued my regular practices of mindfulness and by then yoga, and other tools that were helping me recover and restore my well-being. Later that spring, a year after letting go of my goal of returning to the healthcare profession, I discovered that I still had "emotional baggage" remaining in relation to my time working in the NHS IAPT service. The was also the case regarding the challenges I had experienced during the doctorate, particularly in relation to the lack of support I experienced from the university in connection with the research aspect.

So, understanding the impact unexpressed emotions can have, I embarked on some emotional processing work once more. I returned to journaling again. I wrote and I wrote, and at times I cried, until I had expressed everything I needed to express – all the pent-up frustration, anger, disappointment, sense of powerlessness and all the other emotions I was feeling. It covered pages and pages. At the end of it, I felt drained but also a sense of relief. Afterwards I practised self-kindness and self-compassion, which I felt I needed. In the summer we had a heatwave and so, living by the coast, I subsequently made the most of the opportunity to rest, recharge and have fun with family, friends and our dog Tommy. Taking the time out, following the challenge of processing the past, helped me to put it all behind me and look forward to the future. My husband, Mark, had been taking time out too, to write his first non-fiction book on a subject related to business consulting.

That autumn, just over four years since starting my burnout recovery, Mark asked me to review his book as a part of my role within our company. I spent the following few months copy-editing it for him, working almost full-time for a period of weeks, before we sent it on to a professional copy editor, for a final edit. I realised that not since working for the NHS had I worked so many hours. However, this time I felt not just a regular sense of tiredness but also a sense of satisfaction at the end of each day, rather than complete exhaustion.

I felt engaged in the process. It was aligned with some of my heart-felt values, and certainly did not clash with any of my values. I had energy, not only physically but mentally too. I felt calm and balanced emotionally, even managing to effectively manage my husband's (understandably) strong reactions to some of my feedback.

It dawned on me that for the first time in more than four years I felt fully myself. I felt fully recovered from burnout and back to "normal". It was wonderful. I felt very grateful to my husband for giving me that task, because it was my first proper work-related "test" in years, and I may have drifted on for longer otherwise. Given that there is no objective medical test for burnout, as it is not classified as a medical condition (WHO, 2019), it is of course possible that I recovered from burnout and restored my well-being sooner than I perceived. All I can say here is that this was my authentic and subjective experience. The time spent copy-editing my husband's book is when I perceived I had recovered as I felt well, resilient and able to tackle such a big project.

As a result of finally feeling restored, and inspired by my husband, I felt ready and able to begin writing what eventually became this book. Like the first self-help book I wrote, this one also took me two years to write and publish. However, this is because as well as writing, I ensured I continued to live my other core values, not only supporting my husband in his work (before the pandemic, which resulted in us being furloughed), but also progressing my own area of work that is meaningful to me, namely teaching others about the power of compassion for better health and happiness. I also ensured I spent appropriate amounts of time on other non-work-related activities to sustain my well-being and happiness.

CONCLUSION

The ultimate purpose of this book has been to help people suffering from burnout to restore their well-being and to make this as simple as possible. Additionally, a principle aim of this book has been to equip readers with what they need to implement one of the important elements of burnout recovery reported in the burnout research, namely taking charge of their well-being. Thus, I have provided a way to do this by revealing the five keys to burnout recovery, which included raising your awareness, restoring your body, being true to yourself, being kind to yourself and making your heart sing.

The advantage of these five keys is that they not only enable the reader to discover how I implemented these keys on my own recovery journeys, but also to use them in their own lives and be safe in the knowledge that these are evidence-based too. A number of tips are included with each key, for readers who want to know how to start to implement the key to be able to do so. In addition, this book includes an authentic account of my personal experiences of repeated chronic stress, burnout and recovery. This is provided with the aim of helping readers to learn from my experiences and to hopefully gain insights into their own. It is included to inspire those suffering from burnout to begin to take charge of their own well-being and recovery and provide them with hope to successfully overcome burnout, even if they are experiencing severe work-related burnout too.

I believe in "walking my talk", as the saying goes, as much as possible. Therefore, I continue to put into practice what I have learnt over the years, as described in this book, as part of my commitment to sustaining my well-being and my happiness. I still have perfectionistic and workaholic "tendencies". Nonetheless, I continue to use the strategies included in this book, with an emphasis on practicing self-compassion, which enable me to manage them effectively. My wish is that this book has inspired you to take control of your own well-being and use the keys to help you overcome burnout and restore your well-being. If you have any questions or would like to find out about my burnout recovery programme, please do get in touch (cb@thecompassiondoctor.com).

I wish you all the best with your recovery and look forward to hearing from you.

Dr. Catherine Buchan

BIBLIOGRAPHY

Abedini, N. C., Stack, S.W., Goodman, J.L., & Steinberg, K.P. (2018). "It's not just time off": a framework for understanding factors promoting recovery from burnout among internal medicine residents. *J Grad Med Educ,10,* 26-32.

Alexander, R. et al. (2021). The neuroscience of positive emotions and affect: Implications for cultivating happiness and wellbeing. *Neuroscience and biobehavioural Reviews, 121,* 220-249.

Ames, D. R., Lee, A., & Wazlawek, A. (2017). Interpersonal assertiveness: Inside the balancing act. *Social and Personality Psychology Compass, 11,* 1–16.

Andreou, E. (2015). Narratives of agency in job burnout recovery (Unpublished master's thesis). School of Business and Economics, University of Jyväskylä, Jyväskylä, Finland.

Arman, M., Hammarqvist, A.S., & Rehnsfeldt, A. (2011). Burnout as an existential deficiency-lived experiences of burnout sufferers. *Scandinavian Journal of Caring Sciences, 25 (2),* 294-302.

Assertive. 2020. In Collinsdictionary.com. Retrieved Jan 19, 2020, from https://www.collinsdictionary.com/dictionary/english/assertive.

Authenticity. 2020. In dictionary.cambridge.org. Retrieved Jan 19, 2020, from https://dictionary.cambridge.org/dictionary/english/authenticity.

Autonomy. 2020. In dictionary.cambridge.org. Retrieved Jan 19, 2020, from https://dictionary.cambridge.org/dictionary/english/autonomy.

Bakker, A. B., Demerouti, E., & Burke, R. (2009). Workaholism and relationship quality: A spillover-crossover perspective. *Journal of Occupational Health Psychology, 14,* 23-33.

Barnard, L.K., & Curry, J.F. (2011). Self-compassion: Conceptualizations, correlates, &interventions. *Review of General Psychology, 15 (4),* 289-303.

Baumeister, R. (2019). Stalking the true self through the jungles of authenticity: Problems, contradictions, inconsistencies, disturbing findings - And a possible way forward. *Review of General Psychology, 23,* 143-154.

Baumeister, R. F. (1991). *Meanings of life.* New York: Guilford Press.

Baumeister, R. F., & Leary, M. R. (1995). The need to belong: Desire for interpersonal attachments as a fundamental human motivation. *Psychological Bulletin, 117,* 497-529.

Beaumont, E., Durkin, M., Hollins-Martin, C.J. & Carson. J. (2016). Measuring relationships between self-compassion, compassion fatigue, burnout and well-being in student counsellors and student cognitive behavioural psychotherapists: A quantitative survey. *Counselling and Psychotherapy Research, 16, (1),* 15-23.

Benson, H. (2000). *The relaxation response – Updated and expanded* (25th Anniversary ed.). New York: Avon.

Bernier, D. (1998). A study of coping: successful recovery from severe burnout and other reactions to severe work-related stress. *Work Stress, 12,* 50-65.

Bishop, S. R., Lau, M., Shapiro, S., Carlson, L., Anderson, N. C., Carmody, J., et al. (2004). Mindfulness: A proposed operational definition. *Clinical Psychology: Science and Practice, 11,* 230-241.

Black, D.S. (2011). A brief definition of mindfulness. *Mindfulness Research Guide.* Accessed from http://www.mindfulexperience.org.

Buchan, C. (2008). *22 Boyfriends to Happiness: My story and the seven secrets on how to find true love.* Triniti Press.

Carson, S. H., & Langer, E. J. (2006). Mindfulness and self-acceptance. *Journal of Rational-Emotive & Cognitive-Behavior Therapy, 24,* 29-43.

Casper, W. J., Vaziri, H., Wayne, J. H., DeHauw, S., & Greenhaus, J. (2018). The jingle-jangle of work-nonwork balance: A comprehensive and meta-analytic review of its meaning and measurement. *Journal of Applied Psychology, 103,*182-214.

Cassar. G. & Breitinger, D. (2019). World Economic forum October 2019 https://www.weforum.org/agenda/2019/10/burnout-mental-health-pandemic/

Chan, D.W. (2010). Teacher burnout revisited: Introducing positive intervention approaches based on gratitude and forgiveness. *Educational Research Journal, 25, (2),* 165-186.

Chatman, J. A. (1989). Improving interactional organizational research: A model of person-organization fit. *Academy of Management Review, 14 (3),* 333–349.

Clark, M. A., Michel, J. S., Zhdanova, L., Pui, S. Y., & Baltes, B. B. (2016). All work and no play? A meta-analytic examination of the correlates and outcomes of workaholism. *Journal of Management,* 42 (7), 1836-1873.

Cowden, R.G., & Meyer-Weitz, A. (2016). Self-reflection and self-insight predict resilience and stress in competitive tennis. *Social Behavior and Personality, 44,* 1133-1150.

Curry, O. S., Rowland, L., Van Lissa, C., Zlotowitz, S., McAlaney, J., & Whitehouse, H. (2018). Happy to help? A systematic review and meta-analysis of the effects of performing acts of kindness on the well-being of the actor. *Journal of Experimental Social Psychology, 76,* 320-329.

Deci, E. L., & Ryan, R. M. (1985). *Intrinsic motivation and self-determination in human behavior.* New York, NY: Plenum.

Donahue, E. G., Forest, J., Vallerand, R. J., Lemyre, P.-N., Crevier-Braud, L., & Bergeron, E ´ . (2012). Passion for work and emotional exhaustion: The mediating role of rumination and recovery. *Applied Psychology: Health and Well-Being, 4 (3),* 341-368.

Dreisoerner, A., Junker, N.M., & van Dick, R. (2020). The Relationship Among the Components of Self-compassion: A Pilot Study Using a Compassionate Writing Intervention to Enhance Self-kindness, Common Humanity, and Mindfulness. *Journal of Happiness Studies*, 1-27.

Durkin, M., Beaumont, E., Martin, C. J. H., & Carson, J. (2016). A pilot study exploring the relationship between self-compassion, self-judgement, self-kindness, compassion, professional quality of life and wellbeing among UK community nurses. *Nurse Educ. Today, 46,* 109-114.

Dyer, W. W. (1990). *Pulling your own strings*. Arrow Books.

Edwards, J. R., Caplan, R. D., & Van Harrison, R. (1998). Person-environment fit theory: Conceptual foundations, empirical evidence, and directions for future research. *In C. L. Cooper (Ed.), Theories of organizational stress (pp. 29-67)*. New York: Oxford University Press.

Egan, H., Manzios, M., & Jackson, C. (2017). Health practitioners and the directive towards compassionate healthcare in the UK: exploring the need to educate health practitioners on how to be self-compassionate and mindful alongside mandating compassion towards patients. *Health Prof. Educ., 3,* 61-63. doi: 10.1016/j.hpe.2016.09.002.

Ekstedt, M., & Fagerberg, I. (2005). Lived experiences of the time pre-ceding burnout. *Journal of Advanced Nursing, 49,* 59-67.

Ellis, A. (1996). How I learned to help clients feel better and get better. *Psychotherapy, 22 (1),* 149-151.

Esch, T., & Stefano, G.B. (2005). Love promotes health. *Neuroendocrinology Letters, 26,* 264-267.

Esquivel, M.K. (2020). Nutrition Strategies for Reducing Risk of Burnout Among Physicians and Health Care Professionals. *American Journal of Lifestyle Medicine*. December 2020.

Fjellman-Wiklund, A., Stenlund, T., Steinholtz, K., & Ahlgren, C. (2010). Take charge: Patients' experiences during participation in a rehabilitation programme for burnout. *J Rehabil Med; 42 (5)*: 475-81.

Flett, G. L., Besser, A., Davis, R. A., & Hewitt, P. L. (2003). Dimensions of perfectionism, unconditional self-acceptance, and depression. *Journal of Rational-Emotive and Cognitive-Behavior Therapy, 21,* 119-138.

Fredrickson, B.L., Cohn, M.A., Coffey, K.A., Pek, J., & Finkel, S.M. (2008). Open hearts build lives: Positive emotions, induced through loving-kindness meditation, build consequential personal resources. *Journal of Personality and Social Psychology, 95,* 1045-1062.

Fredrickson, B. L. (2001). The role of positive emotions in positive psychology: the broaden-and-build theory of positive emotions. *Am. Psychol, 56,* 218-226.

Fredrickson, B. L. (1998). What good are positive emotions? *Rev. Gen. Psychol., 2,* 300-319.

Freudenberger, H. J. (1974). Staff burnout. *Journal of Social Issues, 1,* 159-164.

Gerber, M., Schilling, R., Colledge, F., Ludyga, S., Pühse, U., & Brand, S. (2020). More than a simple pastime? The potential of physical activity to moderate the relationship between occupational stress and burnout symptoms. *International Journal of Stress Management, 27,* 53-64.

Germer, C. K., & Neff, K. D. (2013). Self-compassion in clinical practice. *Journal of Clinical Psychology, 69 (8),* 856-867

Girardi, D., De Carlo, A., Dal Corso, L., Andreassen, C. S., & Falco, A. (2019). Is workaholism associated with inflammatory response? The moderating role of work engagement. *Test. Psychometr. Methodol. Appl. Psychol. 26,* 305-322.

Goleman, D. (2001b). Issues in paradigm building. In C. Cherniss & D. Goleman (Eds.), *The emotionally intelligent workplace: How to select for, measure, and improve emotional intelligence in individuals, groups, and organizations* (pp. 13-26). San Francisco: Jossey-Bass.

Gong, Z., Schooler, J. W., Wang, Y., & Tao, M. (2018). Research on the Relationship between Positive Emotions, Psychological Capital and Job Burnout in Enterprises' Employees: Based on the Broaden-and-Build Theory of Positive Emotions. *Canadian Social Science, 14 (5)*, 42-48. doi:https://doi.org/10.3968/10383

Hall, C.W., Row, K. A., Wuensch, K.L., & Godley, K. R. (2013). The role of self-compassion in physical and psychological well-being. *Journal of Psychology, 147*, 311-323.

Hamidi, M. S., Boggild, M. K., & Cheung, A. M. (2016). Running on empty: a review of nutrition and physicians' well-being. *Postgraduate medical journal, 92*, 478-481.

Hätinen, M., Mäkikangas, A., Kinnunen, U., & Pekkonen, M. (2013). Recovery from burnout during a one-year rehabilitation intervention with six-month follow-up: associations with coping strategies. *International Journal of Stress Management, 20*, 364-390.

Haugstvedt, K.T.S, Hallberg, U., Graff-Iversen, S., Sorensen, M., & Haugli, L. (2011). Increased self-awareness in the process of returning to work. *Scand J Caring Sci, 25*, 762-70

Hicks, J. A., Schlegel, R. J., & Newman, G. E. (2019). Introduction to the Special Issue: Authenticity: Novel Insights into a Valued, Yet Elusive, Concept. *Review of General Psychology, 23 (1)*, 3-7.

Holden, C.L., Rollins, P., & Gonzalez, M. (2020). Does how you treat yourself affect your health? The relationship between health-promoting behaviors and self-compassion among a com-munity sample. *Journal of Health Psychology*. Epub ahead of print 19 March 2020. DOI: 10.1177/1359105320912448.

Holford, P. (1997). *The Optimum Nutrition Bible*. Judy Piatkus (Publishers) Ltd.

Inwood, E., & Ferrari, M. (2018). Mechanisms of Change in the Relationship between Self-Compassion, Emotion Regulation, and Mental Health: A Systematic Review. *Applied Psychology: Health and Well-Being*. 10.1111/aphw.1212.

Jackson-Koku, G., & Grime, P. (2019). Emotion regulation and burnout in doctors: a systematic review. Occupational Medicine (Lond), 69, 9-21.

Janssen, M., Heerkens, Y., Kuijer, W., Van Der Heijden, B., & Engels, J. (2018). Effects of Mindfulness-Based Stress Reduction on employees' mental health: A systematic review. *PLoS One, 13(1)*, e0191332.

Jinpa, T. (2015). *A Fearless Heart: How the Courage to be Compassionate can Transform our Lives*. New York: Hudson Street Press.

Joines, V. & Stewart, I. (2002). *Personality Adaptations: A New Guide to Human Understanding in Psychotherapy and Counselling*. Lifespace Publishing.

Joireman, J. A., Parrott, L., & Hammersla, J. (2002). Empathy and the self-absorption paradox: Support for the distinction between self-rumination and self-reflection. *Self and Identity, 1,* 53-65.

Karr, S. (2019). Avoiding physician burnout through physical, emotional, and spiritual energy. *Current Opinion in Cardiology, 34, 94-97.*

Kind. 2020. In Collinsdictionary.com. Retrieved Jan 19, 2020, from https://www.collinsdictionary.com/dictionary/english/kind.

Kooker, B. M., Shoultz, J., & Codier, E. E. (2007). Identifying emotional intelligence in professional nursing practice. *Journal of Professional Nursing, 23,* 30-36.

Kristensen, T. S., Borritz, M., Villadsen, E., & Christensen, K. B. (2005). The Copenhagen Burnout Inventory: A new tool for the assessment of burnout. *Work & Stress, 19* (3), 192-207.

Kristof-Brown, A. L., Zimmerman, R. D., & Johnson, E. C. (2005). Consequences of individual's fit at work: A meta-analysis of person-job, person-organization, person-group, and person-supervisor fit. *Personnel Psychology, 58,* 281-342.

Lai, S. T., & O'Carroll, R. E. (2017). 'The three good things' – The effects of gratitude practice on wellbeing: a randomised controlled trial. *Health Psychol., 26,* 10-18.

Lapa T. A., Madeira, F.M., Viana, J. S., & Pinto-Gouveia, J. (2017). Burnout syndrome and wellbeing in anaesthesiologists: the importance of emotion regulation strategies. *Minerva Anestesiology, 83,* 191-9

Leighton, S. L., & Roye, A. K. (1984). Prevention and self-care for professional burnout. *Family & Community Health: The Journal of Health Promotion & Maintenance, 6*(4), 44-56.

Lunau, T., Bambra, C., Eikemo, T. A., van der Wel, K. A., & Dragano, N. (2014). A balancing act? Work–life balance, health and well-being in European welfare states. *European Journal of Public Health, 24,* 422-427.

McMillan, L.H.W., & O'Driscoll, M.P. (2004). Workaholism and health: Implications for organizations. *Journal of Organizational Change Management, 17,* 509-519.

Martela, F., & Pessi, A. B. (2018). Significant work is about self-realization and broader purpose: Defining the key dimensions of meaningful work. *Frontiers in Psychology, 9,* 363.

Maslach, C., Jackson, S. H., & Leiter, M. P. (1996). *Maslach Burnout Inventory: Manual, 3rd ed.* Palo Alto, CA: Consulting Psychologists Press.

Maslach C. & Leiter, M. P. (2016). Understanding the burnout experience: recent research and its implications for psychiatry. *World Psychiatry, 15,* 103-11.

Maslach, C., & Leiter, M.P. (1997). *The truth about burnout: How organizations cause personal stress and what to do about it.* SanFrancisco: Jossey-Bass.

Matuska, K. M. (2010). Workaholism, life balance, and well-being: A comparative analysis. *Journal of Occupational Science, 17,* 104-111.

Montero-Marín J., García-Campayo J., Fajó-Pascual M., Carrasco J.M., Gascón S., Gili M., & Mayoral-Cleries, F. (2011). Sociodemographic and occupational risk factors associated with the development of different burnout types: the cross-sectional university of Zaragoza study. *BMC Psychiatry* 11, 49. https://doi.org/10.1186/1471-244X-11-49

Morin, A. (2011). Self-awareness part 1: Definition, measures, effects, functions, and antecedents. *Social & Personality Psychology Compass, 5,* 807-823.

Nangle, M.R., Henry, J.D., von Hippel, C., & Kjelsaas, K. (2019). An empirical study of how emotion dysregulation and social cognition relate to occupational burnout in dentistry. *British Dental Journal, 227,* 285-290.

Neff, K. D., Knox, M. C., Long, P., & Gregory, K. (2020). Caring for Others without Losing Yourself: An Adaptation of the Mindful Self-Compassion Program for Healthcare Communities. *Journal of Clinical Psychology, 76, (9).* doi:10.1002/jclp.23007:1-20

Neff, K.D. (2011). Self-compassion, self-esteem, and well-being. *Social and Personality Compass, 5, (1),* 1-12. doi:10.1111/j.1751-9004.2010.00330.x.

Neff, K. D. (2003). Self-compassion: an alternative conceptualization of a healthy attitude toward oneself. *Self and Identity, 2,* 85-102.

Neves, I. C., Amorim, F. F., & Salomon, A.L. R. (2020). Burnout Syndrome on Teachers and its Relation to Nutrition: An Integrative Review. *Current Psychiatry Research and Reviews Formerly: Current Psychiatry Reviews, Vol, 16 (1),* 31-41.

Oerlemans, W. G., & Bakker, A. B. (2014). Burnout and daily recovery: A day reconstruction study. *Journal of Occupational Health Psychology, 19,* 303-314.

Peneva, I., & Mavrodiev, S. (2013). A historical approach to assertiveness. *Psychological Thought, 6 (1)*, 3-26.

Post, M. (1981). *American Public Welfare Association, Vol. 39* (1). Retrieved from: https://www.eccta.org/Forms/Presentations/Conference/2017/Bur noutQuestionnaire_6-21-17.pdf

Poulsen, M.G., Poulsen, A.A., Khan, A., Poulsen, E.E., & Khan, S.R. (2015). Recovery Experience and Burnout in Cancer Workers in Queensland. *European Journal of Oncology Nursing, Vol. 19*, 23-28.

Reddan, M.C., Wager, T.D., & Schiller, D. (2018). Attenuating neural threat expression with imagination. Neuron, 100, 994-1005.

Regedanz, K. (2008). Job burnout recovery. Doctoral dissertation. Institute of Transpersonal Psychology, California.

Richardson, C. M. E., Trusty, W. T., & George, K. A. (2018). Trainee wellness: Self-critical perfectionism, self-compassion, depression, and burnout among doctoral trainees in psychology. *Counselling Psychology Quarterly*. https://doi.org/10.1080/09515 070.2018.15098 39.

Rowland, R., & Curry, O. S. (2018). A range of kindness activities boost happiness. *The Journal of Social Psychology, 159*, 340-343.

Ryan, R. M., & Brown, K. W. (2003). Why we don't need self-esteem: Basic needs, mindfulness, and the authentic self. *Psychological Inquiry, 14*, 71-76.

Ryan, W. S., & Ryan, R. M. (2019). Toward a social psychology of authenticity: Exploring within-person variation in autonomy, congruence, and genuineness using self-determination theory. *Review of General Psychology, 23*, 1-10.

Ryff, C. D. (1995). Psychological well-being in adult life. *Current Directions in Psychological Science, 4*, 99-104.

Ryff, C. D. (1989). Happiness is everything, or is it? Explorations on the meaning of psychological well-being. *Journal of Personality and Social Psychology, 57*, 1069-1081.

Salminen, S., Andreou, E., Holma, J., Pekkonen, M., & Mäkikangas, A. (2017). Narratives of burnout and recovery from an agency perspective: A two-year longitudinal study. *Burnout Research, 7*, 1-9.

Salminen, S., Mäkikangas, A., Hätinen, M., Kinnunen, U., & Pekkonen, M. (2015). My well-being in my own hands: Experiences of beneficial recovery during burnout rehabilitation. *Journal of Occupational Rehabilitation, 25 (4)*, 733-741.

Schaufeli, W. B., Bakker, A. B., Hoogduin, K., Schaap, C., & Kladler, A. (2001). The clinical validity of the Maslach Burnout Inventory and the Burnout Measure. *Psychology and Health, 16*, 565-582.

Schlegel, R. J., Hicks, J. A., King, L. A., & Arndt, J. (2011). Feeling like you know who you are: Perceived true self-knowledge and meaning in life. *Personality and Social Psychology Bulletin, 37*, 745-756.

Siu, O. L., Cooper, C. L., & Phillips, D. R. (2014). Intervention studies on enhancing work well-being, reducing burnout, and improving recovery experiences among Hong Kong health care workers and teachers. *International Journal of Stress Management, 21*, 69-84.

Sonnentag, S. (2001). Work, recovery activities, and individual well-being: A diary study. *Journal of Occupational Health Psychology, 6*, 196-210.

Speed, B. C., Goldstein, B. L., & Goldfried, M. R. (2018). Assertiveness training: A forgotten evidence-based treatment. *Clinical Psychology: Science and Practice, 25*, e12216.

Strümpfer, D. J. W. (2003). Resilience and burnout: A stitch that could save nine. *South African Journal of Psychology, 33*, 69-79.

Sun, J., Wang, Y., Wan, Q., & Huang, Z. (2019). Mindfulness and special education teachers' burnout: The serial multiple mediation effects of self-acceptance and perceived stress. *Soc. Behav. Pers. Int. 47*, 1-8.

Sussman, S. (2012). Workaholism: A review. *Journal of Addiction Research and Therapy, S6,* 4120. doi:10.4172/2155-6105.S6-001

Sutton, A. (2020). Living the good life: A meta-analysis of authenticity, well-being and engagement. *Personality and Individual Differences, 153,* 1-14.

Taris, T. W., Beek I., & Schaufeli, W. B. (2010). Why do perfectionists have a higher burnout risk than others? The mediational effect of workaholism. *Romanian Journal of Applied Psychology, 12,* 1-7.

ten Brummelhuis, L. L., & Bakker, A. B. (2012). A resource perspective on the work-home interface: The work-home resources model. *American Psychologist, 67,* 545-556. http://dx.doi.org/10.1037/a0027974

Thompson, R. W., Arnkoff, D. B., & Glass, C. R. (2011). Conceptualizing mindfulness and acceptance as components of psychological resilience to trauma. *Trauma, Violence & Abuse,12 (4),* 220-235

Thompson, B.L., & Waltz, J.A. (2008). Mindfulness, self-esteem, and unconditional self-acceptance. *Journal of Rationale Emotive Cognitive Behavior Therapy, 26,* 119-126.

Tong, J., Wang, L., & Peng, K. (2015). From person–environment misfit to job burnout: Theoretical extensions. *Journal of Managerial Psychology, 30 (2),* 169-182.

Vallerand, R. J., Blanchard, C., Mageau, G. A., Koestner, R., Ratelle, C., & Leonard, M., et al. (2003). Les passions de l'Âme: On obsessive and harmonious passion. *Journal of Personality and Social Psychology, 85,* 756–767.

Van den Bosch, R., Taris, T.W., Schaufeli, W.B., Peeters, M.C., & Reijseger, G. (2019). Authenticity at work: A matter of fit? *The Journal of Psychology, 153,* 247-266.

Van den Bosch, R., & Taris, T. W. (2014a). Authenticity at work: The development and validation of an individual authenticity measure at work. *Journal of Happiness Studies, 15(1),* 1-18.

Van den Bosch, R., & Taris, T. W. (2014b). The authentic worker's well-being and performance: The relationship between authenticity at work, well-being, and work outcomes. *The Journal of Psychology, 148 (6),* 659-681.

Vlachou, E. M., Damigos, D., Lyrakos, G., Chanopoulos, K., Kosmidis, G., & Karavis, M. (2016). The relationship between burnout syndrome and intelligence in healthcare professionals. *Health Science Journal, 10 (5),* 1-9. doi:10.4172/1791-809X.1000100502.

Wachs, K., & Cordova, J. V. (2007). Mindful relating: Exploring mindfulness and emotion repertoires in intimate relationships. *Journal of Marital and Family Therapy, 33,* 464-481.

Whitefield, C. L. (1987). *Healing the Child Within: Discovery and Recovery for Adult Children of Dysfunctional Families.* Health Communications Inc.

Winwood, P. C., Bakker, A. B., & Winefield, A. H. (2007). An investigation of the role of non-work-time behavior in buffering the effects of work-strain. *Journal of Occupational and Environmental Medicine, 49,* 862-871.

Wood, A. M., Froh, J. J., & Geraghty, A. W. A. (2010). Gratitude and well-being: A review and theoretical integration. *Clinical Psychology Review, 30,* 890-905.

World Health Organisation. (2020, November 26). "Physical Activity". Retrieved from: https://www.who.int/news-room/fact-sheets/detail/physical-activity.

World Health Organisation. (2019, May 28). Burn-out an "occupational phenomenon": International Classification of Diseases. Retrieved from: https://www.who.int/news/item/28-05-2019-burn-out-an-occupational-phenomenon-international-classification-of-diseases.

World Health Organization. (2018). *International classification of diseases for mortality and morbidity statistics* (11th Revision). Retrieved from https://icd.who.int/browse11/l-m/en

Zhang, J. W., Chen, S., Tomova Shakur, T.K., Bilgin, B., Chai, W. J., Ramis, T., Shaban-Azad, H., Razavi, P., Nutankumar, T., & Manukyan, A. (2019). A Compassionate Self Is a True Self? Self-Compassion Promotes Subjective Authenticity. *Pers Soc Psychol Bull, 45 (9),* 1323-1337.

RESOURCES

For inspiring talks, workshops and other events: -

Alternatives
St James's Church
197 Piccadilly
London, W1J 9LL
Tel: 020 7282 6711
www.alternatives.org.uk

For nutritionists or naturopaths: -

BANT (British Association for Nutrition and Lifestyle Medicine
27 Old Gloucester Street
London, WC1N 3XX
Telephone: 01425 462 532
www.bant.org.uk

GCRN (General Council and Register of Naturopaths)
Lytchett House,
13 Freeland Park,
Wareham Road,
Lytchett Matravers,
Poole,
Dorset,
BH16 6FA
Tel: 01458 840072
www.gcrn.org.uk

For psychotherapy or counselling: -

UKCP (UK Council for Psychotherapy)
2 America Square, London, EC3N 2LU
020 7014 9955
www.psychotherapy.org.uk

BACP (British Association for Counselling and Psychotherapy).
15 St John's Business Park
Lutterworth
Leicestershire
LE17 4HB,
United Kingdom
Tel: 01455 883300
www.bacp.co.uk

Author Bio

Dr. Buchan has been involved in the field of psychology for over 16 years. In that time, she has worked in private practice as a psychologist and coach, written a self-help book on finding love and improving relationships and been a voluntary therapist for a substance abuse charity. She has a doctorate in counselling psychology and has also worked as a therapist in the UK's National Health Service (NHS). Catherine now works as *The Compassion Doctor*, teaching others in the UK and internationally, how to reduce stress, overcome anxiety and recover from burnout and experience better well-being and happiness in their lives with the power of compassion.

Catherine lives in the UK with her husband Mark and their rescue dog Tommy. She enjoys travelling around with them in their campervan, spending time in nature, going for long walks, reading and catching up with family and friends in the UK and abroad.

Her website is <u>www.thecompassiondoctor.com</u>.